2ND EDITION

Old Path Preaching Methods

2ND EDITION

Old Path Preaching Methods

RULES OF ENGAGEMENT FOR EFFECTIVE SERMON PREPARATION AND DELIVERY

Dr. James A. Lince

DayStarPublishing

PO Box 464 Miamitown, Ohio 45041

Old Path Preaching Methods Second Edition
Copyright © 2007
Bible Believer's Baptist Church
Jacksonville, Florida

Scripture quotations are from the Authorized King James Version.

Published by DayStar Publishing
PO Box 464 Miamitown, OH 45041
1-800-311-1823 www.daystarpublishing.org

Printed by Faith Baptist Church Publications
3607 Oleander Blvd. Ft. Pierce, FL 34982
1-800-440-5579 www.fbcpublications.com

ISBN: 978-1-890120-44-3
Library of Congress Control Number: 2007927906

THE LORD'S MARINE

God's best soldiers are not honored with earthly medals on their chest.
The Lord must call them front and center to reward them with His best.

So today let us imagine what transpired on Heaven's scene,
As James A. Lince came forward to kneel before the King of Kings.

Close your eyes to see the glory and the joy of the occasion,
As the Lord – a Man of War – presents His soldier with this citation:

"For conspicuous gallantry in the fight for the souls of men –
With intrepidity in action assaulting Satan, Hell, and sin.

Rising from a sheltered position, caring not for your own life –
Forsaking all to follow me, bravely fighting the good fight.

Leading many wounded sinners up the hill called Calvary,
Breaching the enemy's perimeter with a Sword - the KJV.

Through the battlefields of Bridgeport and the post atop Blue Ridge,
The rank and file received support as you preached just what you lived.

In the heat of many battles, enduring conflicts long and hard,
When others were retreating – you shouted - "FIX BAYONETS! CHARGE!!!

When pinned down by adversity never once did you resign,
But prayed "Be Thou My Vision Lord, not my will but Thine."

Rising through the ranks to General, an example to many a man,
Yet submissive as a private in obeying God's commands.

On behalf of your indomitable leadership and selfless devotion to duty,
I summoned the angels in Heaven and ordered - "Bring this soldier to Me."

To present these Medals of Honor, to bestow thy full reward –
James, take your rest beneath my wings in the joys of the Lord.

For rarely down upon the Earth are warriors like you seen.
Let it be known through eternity - Behold, the Lord's Marine!

Let the gold, silver, and precious stones validate this commendation.
Well done, my good and faithful son! Signed - *The Captain of Salvation*

So each time that we remember him, let us keep this scene in mind.
For it's not a fallen soldier that we have left behind.

It's the day of his commissioning although tears still fill our eyes.
So Brother Jim until we meet again we bid you - SEMPER FI.

IN MEMORY AND HONOR OF DR. JAMES A. LINCE
1950-2005 (RUTH 2:12)

Table of Contents

Foreword

It is my privilege to write a few words about the book *Old Path Preaching Methods* and its author – Dr. James A. Lince. He has been my good friend for many years. When I consider his ministry, there are many things that I can say about him.

Dr. Lince is an excellent teacher and student of the Bible. As the pastor of Bridgeport Baptist Church and the founder of Blue Ridge Bible Institute, he has trained many men in the scriptures and prepared them for the ministry. However, Dr. Lince is primarily and preeminently a preacher. In fact, I consider him to be one of the greatest preachers of our time. I do not give him that kind of credit just because he is my friend. I say that because I know it is a true statement. God has blessed him with the abilities and talents of a great preacher. I've seen the Lord use him in a mighty way to accomplish His will in the declaration of the word of God.

Like a master in any type of craft, Dr. Lince has fine-tuned and polished his preaching skills over the years. He has given and applied himself to learn and master the art of preaching. When it comes to preaching, we understand that a preacher is self-made in the sense that he must constantly apply himself to the work and the ministry that God called him to do. However, we also know that a preacher is God-made. The Lord will fashion a man so that he can glorify Himself through the life and the preaching of His preacher. As you read and study this book, you will benefit from the vast knowledge and experience Dr. Lince has gathered over the course of twenty-fives years in the ministry – a ministry which has faithfully exalted the name of the Lord Jesus Christ.

As an eyewitness of Dr. Lince's life, I can say that I have seen God make the man through trials and tribulations – **"a vessel unto honour, sanctified, and meet for the master's use"** (II Timothy 2:21). In my many preaching experiences with Dr. Lince, I've seen his preaching reveal not only the human side of the message, but also the Divine side, which is the power of the Holy Spirit on the man and the message he delivers. That kind of preaching results in the salvation of lost souls. It also moves human hearts towards God in submission to His will. My purpose here is not to heap praise and accolades upon Dr. Lince. Instead, I want to convey to the reader that here is a man who fully understands what preaching is. He has learned it through experience over time. And this writing is based on those years of knowledge and expertise, which Dr. Lince is endeavoring to pass along to the next generation of preachers.

As pointed out in this book, we are living in a day described by the Apostle Paul in II Timothy 4:3, **"For the time will come when they will not endure sound doctrine; but after their own lusts shall they heap to themselves teachers, having itching ears."** We are living in these final days in which the Bible teacher is preeminent – not the Bible preacher. Certainly, there is still a need for teaching and the teacher. The Bible makes that clear. However, the need of the hour is PREACHING. The need is no different today than in the former days and dispensations gone by. The generations that experienced the greatest moves of God in their midst were those where great preachers walked among them. The great preachers of the olden days were John Wesley, George Whitfield, Dwight L. Moody, Billy Sunday, Sam Jones, and Bob Jones Sr.; names that still live on to the present generation. Others who were lesser known may have been forgotten with time, but their records and exploits are recorded in the annals of Glory never to be forgotten. We may be in the final stages of the Laodicean Church period and much of

Christianity may be going the way of apostasy and heresy, but God is still looking for some preachers; men who with trumpet voice and clarion call will sound forth the wonderful message of salvation and the great truths of "thus saith the Lord."

So, if you are a young man who has been called by God to be a preacher and are in need of instruction, or if you're a preacher who is interested in training men who have been called to preach under your ministry, or if you are a veteran preacher who is simply looking for a good book on the subject of preaching, Dr. Lince has written this book for you.

It is written:

1. Purposefully – in that the author stays true to the title and theme of his book.
2. Practically – with regard to its readability and application of its various subjects.
3. Plentifully – in that it contains a wealth of information with regard to instruction and application as the author draws from many outside sources as well as his own personal experiences.
4. Personally – in that as you read this volume, the author's heart, mind, and person are revealed.

The greatest joy of every preacher is to be used by God. This includes seeing souls saved, the saints edified and encouraged in the things of God, the church revived, and men called into the preaching ministry. "Like produces like" or as it is stated many times in the first chapter of Genesis, "after their kind." This volume was penned by a great preacher. May it be used by God to produce another generation of preachers after his kind.

Dr. Vince Massa
Landmark Baptist Church
Stamford, Connecticut
January 2005

Introduction

"There are not many things in this world that I truly know, but what I know is worth knowing." Those were the words of my late Grandfather, John Melbourne Lince (1899-1980). I heard him make that statement many times as I was growing up.

He was a man that lived inside of his heart. Grandpa truly had a big heart. I was fully grown before I came to realize how big his heart really was. Although Grandpa was not saved when I was young, he sure did have a bushel full of common sense.

Now the preacher in the family happened to be Grandpa's older brother (my great Uncle), Dr. Harry Lince (1885-1958). He was an associate to the great preacher J. Frank Norris back in the days of the old Grand River Church. After the split of Norris and G.B. Vick, my Uncle Harry went and started his own work for the Lord. I can still remember going to hear Uncle Harry preach when I was a young boy staying over at my Grandparent's house – but there was more than preaching going on. I later found out that my Grandma Lince, along with my Uncle Harry and Aunt Martha, had spent many hours back then in prayer over my soul. They were Christian relatives who always treated me good and expressed their concern for me through prayer. When I trusted Christ on August 14, 1975, their prayers for me were answered and perhaps more so than they ever thought would be, especially when I became an independent Baptist preacher two months later, in October 1976.

However, their prayers for me were not the only ones God answered. Four years later, in 1979, I experienced one of the greatest joys of my Christian life – the privilege of leading my Grandpa Lince to the Lord. He ended up getting baptized in a country church near the lake where he lived. I don't know why it took Grandpa until the year before he left us to get saved, but what I do know is that he got saved. What I find interesting is that although he spent practically his entire life as a lost man, he seems to have had a better knowledge and appreciation of God's holiness than a lot of Christians. He once told me that he thought God wouldn't save him because of the one time he had looked at a "dirty book" while working as a truck driver. That said something to me about the kind of character the man had and the way he thought. So when I recall how he used to say *"There are not many things in this world that I truly know, but what I know is worth knowing,"* I believe that he really did _know_ what he was talking about.

I heard him make that statement many times as I was growing up. And after spending the past twenty-nine years as a preacher, I have developed my own rendition of Grandpa's adage, which leads me to say this – I myself do not know many things in this world, but I do know something about preaching. I can say that because I have studied preachers and preaching over the length of my ministry. I've taught preachers here at Blue Ridge Bible Institute (BRBI) since 1986. I've spent many hours counseling with preachers (both the young and not so young) as they struggled with their call to the ministry. I've watched preachers forsake all, sacrifice everything, and do their best in the work of the Lord. I've also seen preachers enter the ministry with good intentions, but the spiritual pressure became so great that they eventually gave up, dropped out, and quit. I've listened to those who can preach and to those who can't preach. I've watched them rise and I've watched them fall. Yes, I know preachers. I've seen them come and I've certainly watched them go.

After all these years in the ministry, and with all the time I've spent training these men for the work, I believe that preachers can typically be placed into one of the three following categories:

- Those who won't preach. They must be forced out of the pulpits.
- Those who can preach. Such are few and far between.
- Those who can't preach. They have either never been called or they have never been taught.[1]

And it is for the benefit of this last category of preachers that I've set out to write this book.

Over the years I have noticed a decline of preaching within the "Bible believing" crowd. Many preachers today have traded in their God given gift to preach for some other form of delivery. Some prefer to conduct Bible studies, where the emphasis is upon TEACHING and OUTREACHING, but not PREACHING. Others utilize perhaps a more sophisticated approach as they attempt to "engage" their church members with expositions on the deeper learning of the scriptures. Well, regardless of which method a so-called preacher man may prefer to use, we know for certain that God's man must implement God's method if sinners are going to be saved and saints are going to be straightened out. God's method is and has always been **"the foolishness of preaching"** (1 Corinthians 1:21). Anything else amounts to mere lunacy.

Now much of the problem we see today results from the fact that preachers are not being taught how to do their job, which is to preach. This is because many people fail to consider the fact that preaching (like any profession) demands not only work but training, instruction, and the application of basic skills. In other words, there is a level of education required if a man is going to preach and do it right. However, there are still those who insist that preaching cannot and should not be taught at all. This is particularly a problem in the South, a/k/a "the Bible belt." For some reason or another, many southerners were raised to believe (and remain convinced) that preaching means nothing more than to "take a verse and take a fit." No preparation required, just open the book and have at it. Those who hold to this idea often view preaching as some strange ability to entertain a congregation simply by ranting and raving for an hour without ever stopping to catch a breath. To these folks, it doesn't seem to matter what a preacher says from a *doctrinal* standpoint, but only how a preacher *delivers* the message. That is a very dangerous misconception. Nonetheless, there are many saved Christians who view loud and long preaching as a supernatural talent given to them by God that never requires any kind of learning, study, or preparation. I suppose that is why in many areas it is considered blasphemy to suggest trying to teach someone how to preach.

Conversely, in the North, we find almost the exact opposite scenario. In that part of the country, education is considered not only the key to knowledge, but also the doorway to becoming a preacher. In the North, preaching is often looked upon as a profession, nothing more than a job or a career. This view demeans the work of the ministry just as much as the "take a verse, take a fit" approach found in the South.

Don't misunderstand what I am saying. I do believe that gifts for preaching are given by God, but I also believe that those gifts, or skills, must also be developed. It has been said that becoming a good preacher is a lot like eating an elephant, you can't eat it all at one time, but you can eat the whole thing piece by piece. Make no mistake about it, that's how preaching is. One of the greatest tragedies I have ever seen is a young preacher who gets the calling and the next thing you know he becomes a legend in his own mind by truly believing that he is a complete and finished preacher. Nothing could be farther from the truth. As E.M. Bounds pointed out in his book *Power through Prayer,* "It takes twenty years to make a man, and it takes twenty years to make a message."[2]   Let me tell you, that statement is exactly right!! Now if you had told me such a thing twenty-nine years ago, when I first started out on the sawdust trail of my own ego, I would have told you that such a statement was foolishness. You know, just some old preacher trying to control us younger God-called preachers. I have come to know better and so should you. None of us have arrived as far as preaching is concerned.

Yet, we are stewards of what God has entrusted us with. God gives us the gift and the skill. Then He holds us accountable for our stewardship. We are ever learning, growing, and sharpening our tools for this calling. Although we will never attain perfection, we must always persist in trying to learn how to preach to the best of our ability. With each passing year, I've become increasingly convinced that skills development is the essential key to becoming a better preacher.

That is why I have written this book on what I consider to be the rules of engagement for effective preparation and sermon delivery. I refer to it as "old path" preaching methods. You will also hear it referred to from time to time as the "old shoe" method. It is my desire to help preachers (both young and old) to lay hold of this great old-fashioned manner of preaching.

Essentially, there are only two ways to approach this important undertaking called preaching: 1) there is man's way and 2) there is God's way. Man's way usually relies on impressing other men with education, knowledge, and modern-day psychology. Man's method typically requires programs, special events, contemporary music, passion plays, performances, movies, game nights and a hundred other different techniques to bring people in and entertain them under the guise of a spiritual church service. My friends, that's not God's way. The Bible clearly points out that <u>preaching</u> is God's preferred manner of drawing lost sinners unto Him. Note 1 Corinthians 1:21:

… it <u>pleased</u> God by the foolishness of preaching to save them that believe.

Preaching is what pleases God. The emphasis in our churches must be on preaching if we are to please God; and not just any old kind of preaching. I believe that the Bible clearly reveals the way it should be done. It is the preaching that adds souls to the body of Christ and edifies the saints. It is preaching done from the right book. It is the preaching that has brought millions into the kingdom of God over the centuries.

At the beginning of the Church Age, we see the method given to us by the New Testament apostles and even the Lord Himself. It was the Apostle Paul's method as well. Their preaching was simple, straightforward, and easy enough for even a child to grasp. It spoke to the heart of the common man. At times it came across as rude, but it was always relevant. At other times it appeared coarse, but it was consistently convicting. It is a preaching method that has continued down through the generations. It was the preaching style embraced by the Albigenses, the Henricians, the Waldenses, the Paulicians, and the Lollards. It was the preferred method of Savanarola, Huss, Luther, and Zwingle. It was God's kind of preaching. It frustrated the papacy the same way it did the Pharisees. It infuriated the Nicolaitans while at the same time it encouraged the needy, lifted up the wretched, and straightened out the sinners. Such preaching was (and still is) derived from a fruitful seed – the word of God. It is preaching that was watered by the blood of martyrs and tempered by the fires of Smithfield. This preaching produced the Great Awakening and spawned other great spiritual movements across the world. The Holy Spirit empowered the adherents of the old path preaching method; men such as George Whitfield, Jonathan Edwards, John and Charles Wesley. Others continued along this path; preachers we recognize from the not too distant past such as Dwight L. Moody, Charles Spurgeon, Mordecai Ham, and Billy Sunday.

It is no wonder that these men were great preachers. The Bible pointed these men in the direction that they chose to follow. It is the same path that we (as preachers) should continue following today:

Stand ye in the ways, and see, and ask for the old paths, where is the good way, and walk therein. And ye shall find rest for your souls.
Jeremiah 6:16

Brethren, that verse expresses my sincere desire. We are not out to establish a new way. Our mainstay is in that old time religion, which is preaching Jesus Christ and him crucified. That is the direction that we must pursue. I hope to point you in that direction. It is a good way because it is the Lord's way. His way is always the best way. Let's tread down this path together.

Moving forward, we will address very important topics and key areas concerning what it means to preach from the old paths and to preach effectively. Where do we begin? First of all, we will examine the call to preach. How do you even know that you've been called? Can you answer that question? There are other important considerations that must also be addressed.   For example, do you have a preacher's heart? What are the priorities when it comes to preaching the word of God? What about leadership?

This book also examines the essential ingredients of doctrinally sound, Bible-based old path preaching. Moreover, it lays out a plan that can be used to build expository sermons. We will combine this approach with the mechanics of old-fashioned common sense delivery that will minister to the common people.

I will also relate a few of the experiences that I've gone through (and observations I've made) throughout my many years of being a pastor. I'll discuss not only what pastoral leadership is, but also what it is not.   These gems on leadership are intended to give you a few helpful hints that I hope will be beneficial to you in the years to come as you continue preaching and working in the ministry.

Gentlemen, there are many challenges, disappointments, and setbacks that a preacher will face, but there is nothing like the joy of knowing that you are being used of God as a vessel to preach His word and make an everlasting impact upon the eternal souls of men.

1

The Call of the Preacher –
PART ONE: The Spiritual & Biblical Tests

The _call_ of the preacher is the most important and essential component of being an effective preacher. The truth about the call to preach is found in the Bible. It is imperative to understand this truth if you believe that God is calling you to be a preacher. The truth about the call to preach is not a deep, dark mystery that is covered up in the scriptures. A man can know how God deals with men whom He has called to the ministry.

First of all, let me say that a man who is called to preach must know that he has truly been called of God and his calling must line up with the truths found in the Bible. If so, such a man must set his sights on learning about preaching. However, if a man is not called, then he must set out to find some other area of service that he can do for the glory of God. Remember, preaching is not simply something that you do – it is something that you are. It is serious business and it involves much trial and tribulation. I can assure you that preaching is complicated enough with the call of God upon your life. I cannot imagine preaching without the call of God as a means of earning a paycheck. You surely don't want to get into anything like preaching without a divine calling. So, if God has called you to preach, praise God; and if he hasn't called you to preach, then praise God.

The call to preach is indeed a biblical truth. As I mentioned, this truth about the calling of God isn't hidden in the Bible. It is a truth that is plainly set before our eyes. In the most basic sense of the word, the Bible indicates that all Christians are called ones.[1] Here, I am referring to a basic calling, which is the call to receive the Lord Jesus Christ as our personal Saviour (Ephesians1:18, 4:1, 2 Timothy 1:9, Hebrews 3:1, 2 Peter 1:10).

There is also God's call to the Christian with regard to **"good works"** as the Bible points out in Ephesians 2:10. In 1 Timothy 6:18, the Bible says **"that they do good, that they be rich in good works, ready to distribute, willing to communicate."** In Titus 2:7, Paul wrote, **"In all things shewing thyself a pattern of good works: in doctrine shewing uncorruptness, gravity, sincerity."** These passages refer to the call that every Christian has upon their life. The Pauline doctrine makes it clear that Christians are to be a people **"zealous of good works"** (Titus 2:14). Included in these good works would be the call to preach.

There are several examples of how God calls a man. In the Old Testament, we can read about the call of Moses in Exodus 3:4-22. When God called Moses, He spoke out of a burning bush. Now what kind of a bush was it that God used? The Bible doesn't tell us anything about it. And there is a reason why. The reason is because any old bush will do. What am I saying? I'm saying that it doesn't matter if a man who is called to preach has talent. That's not the main thing. What does matter is whether or not that man has God. The call of Moses gives us a great example. God was not looking for a great speaker or a man of prominence. God was looking for a man that He could use.

Moses was the first man in the Bible with a formal call of God to engage in God's service. God also called him to be a true leader. What made Moses the man he was? It was God's call upon his life. In order to make a few practical applications about the call to the ministry, let's review what we learn from the life of Moses.

   1. Training of the natural man avails nothing in the work of God. Although Moses was undoubtedly brought up in the wisdom of Egypt and the best education that royalty could provide, this offered little to no value when it came to fulfilling God's commission to lead the children of Israel out of bondage. Moses had to rely solely on the wisdom of God's word. Yes, Moses had spent forty years in the Egyptian courts. However, when the Lord appeared to him in the land of Midian as he watched over the sheepfolds on the backside of the desert, the first leader of Israel was full of unbelief and self-will. His formal education did not change that.

   2. God individually prepares His servants. God dealt personally and directly with Moses, the man He was going to honor as His ambassador. This has always been, and still is, the vital prerequisite for effectiveness in God's service. The man that God uses must have a personal knowledge of God from his own personal experience. It is a knowledge obtained by the direct revelation of God to the soul. This comes with a definite call from God that warrants the man to engage in His service. The man recognizes the difficulties confronting him, but will confidently rest on God's promises for ultimate success.

   3. The Lord endows His servants for the work they are called to do. In the life of Moses, this endowment bestowed power upon him to work three miracles. The first two signs were designed to teach him an important lesson as a servant of God. Moses was shown the secret of overcoming Satan and he was also reminded of the corruption of his own heart. These are things that every servant must see. The third miracle, or sign, was given to show the judgment awaiting those who rejected God's word.

4. God doesn't expect perfection in the man He calls. Like many other men that God has called, Moses thought that perfection was required before he could be used as a servant of God. Moses had the same problems many men have with regard to leadership.

- Self-occupation (Exodus 3:11)
- Fear (Exodus 3:13)
- Unbelief (Exodus 4:1)
- Pride (Exodus 4:10)

Like Moses, many men suppose that the gift of oratory is a prime pre-requisite for an effective ministry. The misconception today is that those who are being "trained for the ministry" must have a course in rhetoric and elocution. It's as though we think that men who are dead in sins can be quickened by the enticing words of men's wisdom. Have we become foolish enough to believe that such carnal weapons could ever have a place in spiritual warfare? It is sad that such elementary spiritual matters are so little understood in this 21st century. It seems that we have forgotten what Paul told us in 1 Corinthians 2:1:

> **And I, brethren, when I came to you, <u>came not with</u> excellency of speech or of wisdom, declaring unto you the testimony of God.**

Paul and Moses were not eloquent speakers, yet God used them both mightily. God knew that He could use him. Looking back at Moses' example, we know from the scripture that Moses did not consider himself capable of speaking for the Lord. Yet, God assured him in Exodus 4:12:

> **Now therefore go, and I will be thy mouth, and teach thee what thou shalt say.**

In that verse, God told Moses that He would give him the words he would need to refute the most eloquent orator of worldly wisdom. It is no wonder that God's blessing has long since departed from the vast majority of our pulpits today. We have stopped too long to examine the training of those who occupy the pulpits. Gentlemen, all the schooling and learning in the world avails nothing unless the Lord is with the mouth of the preacher. Eloquence and rhetorical devices are needless and useless if the Lord is not giving you the words to teach and to preach. God will prepare you and equip you individually if He has called you to the work of the ministry. The Lord will endow you with all that you need to accomplish whatever it is that He has given you to do. These are practical and very valuable truths that we must consider from the calling of Moses.

There are other great Old Testament examples of God calling men. Read about the call of Samuel in 1 Samuel 3:4 or Jeremiah in Jeremiah 1:4-10. In the New Testament, we can read about the calling of the disciples in Mark 3:13-19 or of Barnabas in Acts 13:2. The calling of Paul is mentioned in several passages: Romans 1:1; 1 Corinthians 1:1; and Galatians 1:15.

Olford on the call to preach:

> The call to preach must not be confused with the desire to serve as an elder or deacon (see 1 Tim. 3:1). . . The call to preach must not be conditioned by the need for the gospel . . . The call to preach must not be controlled by the church, even though the elders of a local church are expected to confirm the call (1 Tim. 4:14; 2 Tim. 1:6).[2]

Olford quoting Wiersbe:

> If God calls you, believe what He says and obey Him. You may not feel up to it, but your adequacy comes from God, not from yourself.[3]

Many years ago, I heard a wise old preacher make a few observations about God's calling to the ministry. He said that whenever a man is called to preach, there are typically a few indications, which, although not infallible, are certainly worth considering, especially if a man finds himself asking, "Am I called to preach?" Although a man may not experience all five of these "signs" (if you will), he will certainly experience at least three of them. They are listed below:

> 1. An interest in the Bible because he wants to help someone. (Note: Not to prove how smart he is or how well he knows the Bible.)
> 2. A total inability to keep his mouth shut when any type of religious question pops up anywhere.
> 3. A real burden to get people saved so that they will not have to go to Hell (which he believes in, having believed what Jesus Christ said about it: Matthew 13:50, 25:41; Mark 9:46-48).
> 4. An ability to enjoy or succeed in any number of jobs that are not the ministry.
> 5. Opportunities to preach constantly open to him. These may only be prison sermons, messages given in nursing homes, little things like teaching Vacation Bible School or preaching on the street, but there will be occasional open doors (1 Corinthians 16:9).[4]

These indications are strong evidence that God may be calling you to preach.

With that said, I believe that every man that God calls to preach will have three things: 1) a divine commission behind him, 2) a divine summons before him, and 3) a divine conviction within him. Now if God has called you to preach, what more could any man ask for or need? Time and time again young men and even preachers have asked me to explain the call to preach. They want the assurance that God really has called them to preach. They want to know about the conviction that they should have or feel. There is no easy answer.

We are all different. Every man possesses different temperaments, different talents, and different training. Yet, one thing is certain. If a man is indwelt and compelled by the living Son of God, there can be no doubt about the call. Using down home terms, I refer to this call to preach as an itch you can't scratch. It's difficult to grasp for many and it is perhaps even more difficult to explain.

As I see it, there are two tests with regard to the call of preaching upon the hearts of men. Notice! I did say <u>men.</u> God never has called a woman to preach. That is not a reference that I have to defend, it is a biblical doctrine that I believe and preach! Read 1 Timothy 2:12.

Now the two tests of the calling upon a man's life are these:

- The spiritual test.
- The biblical test.

The Spiritual Test

Dr. Martyn Lloyd Jones gives us a great example of what to consider when it comes to testing, or finding evidence for the call of God in spiritual terms.   He reminds us that preaching is indeed a spiritual endeavor.   Whenever a man preaches, he is engaged in a spiritual battle for the souls of men and things eternal. Dr. Martyn Lloyd-Jones tells us of this spiritual experience from a preacher's perspective. He wrote:

> The Preacher is a man who is possessed and he is aware of this. I do not hesitate to make this assertion. I would say that I only begin to know something about preaching on those occasions when, as it were, I am looking on, I am speaking, but I am really a spectator. I am amazed at what is happening. I am listening, and I am looking on in utter astonishment, for I am doing it. It is true preaching when I am conscious that I am being used; in the sense that I am as much a spectator as the people that are listening to me. There is this consciousness that is outside me, and yet I am involved in it. I am merely the instrument and the vehicle and the channel of all this.[5]

I can recall one time in my own personal experience when this realization and spiritual awareness in my preaching was as strong as my conviction on the doctrine of eternal security. It happened back during the mid-1980s. Although I really can't recall the exact date or year, I distinctly remember going down to preach at Bethel Children's Home in Lucedale, Mississippi with a few men from our church. We made this trip about once every year. I still consider those meetings in Mississippi as some of the best in my ministry. It was a time of intense spiritual warfare in the United States. The government was coming down against the children's homes of America. Lester Roloff, Levi Wisner, and Herman Fountain were under attack, but they stood their ground. As a result, the Holy Spirit of God was so strong in those places you couldn't miss Him with a missing stick.

I recall one certain meeting that started with the girls from Mack Ford's Children's Home singing. When I was called on to preach, I did so for about 10 minutes. Then I began to experience the power and unction of the Holy Spirit in a way that I never had before. I knew it was me preaching, but in a spiritual sense it was as though I was "the voice crying in the wilderness." I should have been taking notes on myself that night. I had to stop after about ten minutes lest I died that very evening. It was a supernatural moment in my ministry. The message was brought forth to the people and I was thankful. I was also enlightened as to what real preaching actually is. That night God made my calling so very real to me. It was that experience that embedded preaching into my heart. I was addicted (as Paul said) to the ministering of the saints.

That night I felt as though I had passed the test. So, you might ask, "What is the spiritual test?" It is the spiritual realization that God is using you. He is not only speaking to you about the messages to preach, He is also speaking through you when you preach them. For me, it was as plain and as certain as the fact that the King James Bible is the pure word of God.

The Biblical Test

Any man who is questioning whether or not he is called to preach must first look to the Bible as his final authority. Never base your decision to be a preacher on emotion or feelings. Never judge your calling on the fact that Pa or Grandpa was a preacher or the fact that Mother would be disappointed if you didn't turn out to be a preacher. The family tree is a poor excuse for entering the ministry. Just because your daddy or granddaddy was a preacher doesn't mean that you too are called to preach. We're not talking about keeping the family business going or learning a trade. We're talking about God calling a man to preach. Therefore, the first place you should turn to is the Bible. Any man who is questioning God's call upon his life should be persuaded in his own heart and mind. Olford in *Anointed Expository Preaching* (pages 13-14) gives the following questions you should ask yourself:

1) Do I meet the qualifications of a preacher as set forth in the word of God? The qualifications are found in Acts 9:15-29, Acts 22:14-15, and Acts 26:16-18. In these verses we see that God had clearly spoken to Paul. God made it clear that Paul was a chosen vessel to preach the word of God.

2) Have I the witness of the Spirit in my heart that God has called me? The same Spirit that tells me that I am born of God is the same Spirit that witnesses to me concerning my call to preach. This is evident in Romans 8:14, where the Bible says, **"For as many as are led by the Spirit of God, they are the sons of God."** It is the same Spirit that leads a man to become a preacher. If you are called to be a preacher, it will be according to God's purpose and God's grace. It is not according to flesh and blood. It is a spiritual calling in a man's heart and soul. This is what Paul spoke of in Galatians 1:15-16 and also in 2 Timothy 1:8-11.

3) <u>Has the gift of preaching become evident in my life of service?</u> You may find yourself with opportunities to present the word of God to others. It may be in a Sunday school class, a nursing home, a jail, or on a street corner. Regardless of where it is, God will put opportunities in your life to proclaim the word of God and to manifest this gift that He has given you (1 Corinthians 12:7). Is there evidence of that in your life?

4) <u>Has God used my preaching gift to bring salvation to lost souls and to edify the saints?</u> These are the two main objectives that a preacher should strive for. If God has called you to preach, the purpose is to benefit others; either to win them to the Lord Jesus Christ or to minister to the saved ones who are already in His body. Is that what your preaching does? It is not about preaching for results, but preaching with a purpose, which is to lift up the name of our Saviour (John 3:14-15).

Once a man has settled these four very important questions in his heart and mind, he must then ask himself if he is prepared to accept the responsibilities that must be shouldered by a preacher. There are three highly important qualities that we, as preachers, must recognize and employ in our preaching.

- Must Be Faithful in our Preaching.
- We Must Be Fearless in our Preaching.
- We Must Be Fervent in our Preaching.[6]

One of the great preachers of days gone by was G. Campbell Morgan. He referred to these qualities as "truth-clarity-passion."[7] They are accepted principles of preaching that effective preachers have recognized throughout the centuries. "The old masters called it logos-ethos-pathos."[8] We find these same attributes in the New Testament preachers. Paul was faithful in his call to the ministry, in spite of the setbacks and the personal difficulties that tested him throughout his Christian life (2 Timothy 4:4). What greater example of a fearless preacher can we find than Stephen, a man who refused to back down even as the crowd of stiff-necked unbelievers gnashed on him with their teeth (Acts 7:54). And then there was Peter, whose fervent style of preaching resulted in the salvation of three thousand souls in one day (Acts 2:41). These are biblical examples of men that God not only called, but used. They were men and they were sinners, just like you and me. More importantly, they were saved men who were faithful, fearless, and fervent in their call to preach. A man who is called to preach must determine in his heart that he will follow the good examples that God has given us and never let the colors of the blood stained banner fall to the Earth.

Does it require courage? Yes, because the right kind of preaching inevitably leads to persecution. William Tyndale, a great preacher who stood against Rome, who was known as the father of our English Bible, found this to be true in his own life. He left us with an astute observation of what true preaching really means:

> Nay, some will say, a man might preach long enough without persecution, yea, and get favor too, if he would not meddle with the pope, bishops, prelates, and holy ghostly people that live in contemplation and solitariness, nor with great men of the world. I answer, true preaching is salting; and all that is corrupt must be salted; and those persons are of all others most corrupt, and therefore may not be left untouched.[9]

2

The Call of the Preacher –
PART TWO: The Process

When God calls a man to preach there is a process involved. God performs the work on a man throughout this process. Since He has called you, He will do the work. When God is working on a preacher the process can be described as threefold:

- The Taking of a Man.
- The Making of a Man.
- The Breaking of a Man.

The Taking of a Man

The taking of the man is simply the call to preach. God calls different men from different backgrounds. Moses, for example, was a cultured man. He was accustomed to the finer things of life. As a young man in Egypt, he lived among the earthly splendors of Pharaoh's palace. Although God called Moses later in life from the backside of the desert, we should not forget that his early years were spent in the culture of Egypt. He had experienced the best that this world had to offer.

In contrast, we find Amos who was also a prophet, but he came from a very different background. Amos was not from high society. Moses came from a palace whereas Amos came from a pasture. Amos was a common man. He was a herdman and a gatherer of sycamore fruit. Today we would recognize him as a farmer, a man who takes care of livestock and works in the field growing crops.

In the New Testament there is Paul. He is an educated man who studied under Gamaliel, a respected figure during that time. Sitting under this teacher, Paul would not only have learned the pharisaic law, but he would have also been heavily exposed to Greek culture and literature. Paul was lectured and taught by men that were considered the greatest minds of their day – doctors, scholars, philosophers, and the rabbinical priests. Yet, Paul was not limited by his upbringing.[1] Not only did he know how to work with his head, he also knew how to work with his hands as a tentmaker. Paul gives us an example of a man that God called who possessed a significant degree of versatility in his abilities and background.

Then there was Peter. He was an everyday kind of man. As a fisherman, we know that he was a laborer and a hard worker. But, with Peter, we also find many common examples of our own human nature. At times he was aggressive and impatient and at other times he was full of affection and concern. At times he demonstrated great faith and courage, but he is also the apostle who is remembered for denying the Lord. Peter appeared to have great spiritual insight at one moment, but at the next moment would find himself being rebuked by the Lord. Nonetheless, Peter was a man that God called to preach and was used mightily by the Lord.

There are other and more recent examples of preachers that we can consider in order to show how God takes men from different backgrounds and stations in life to use them for his own purposes.   There was D.L. Moody, who was an uneducated man. Yet, we also see R. A. Torry, who had a college education. Men like Charles and John Wesley, Charles Spurgeon, and Bob Jones Sr. each came from Christian homes and backgrounds. They were brought up right and clean. They came from moral families where they grew up hearing the Bible taught and they understood its importance in their lives. But the call to preach does not depend on whether or not a man has a moral background. We know this from other examples of men that God has used.

I'm referring to men such as Billy Sunday and Oliver B. Green. These are men who God also called in spite of their sinful past. These men knew what sin was from their own experience. God did not call these men to preach because they were Sunday school graduates or because of their moral backgrounds. Like Amos, they too could say, **"I was no prophet, neither was I a prophet's son"** (Amos 7:14). Yet, they were men that God <u>took</u> to be preachers because He had a purpose and a plan for their life.

All of these examples make it clear that your background makes no difference to God if He has called you to preach. And your background will not determine the degree to which God can use you. Whether you were raised in a Christian home or in the backstreets and the bars is not the determining factor. Although I will say that the people a man can minister to will usually match the background he is familiar with because he will know how to capture their ear. Nonetheless, what matters most when it comes to God's calling is how willing a man is to submit himself to God. That's really the most important factor.

General Call

Now this call that God has placed upon your life is a general call. When God called you, He called you to preach. So, in that context, your call is the same as mine, which is to be a preacher. This means that we, as preachers, all have one thing in common regardless of our backgrounds. We each have a general call from God to preach. At this point you need to make sure that you understand a couple of things.

First of all, the general call to preach is NOT the same thing as the call to minister. They are two different callings. They are not to be confused as being the same thing. In Ephesians 4:11-12, the Bible differentiates between the gifted men in verse eleven and the men in verse twelve who were called to perform the perfecting of the saints, the work of the ministry, and the edification of the body. Based on these verses, we see that although we may all have the same general call to preach, we do not all have the same call to minister. This will require you to figure out just what God wants you to do in terms of the ministry. Although God has given you a general call, you must now desire to know the truth about how He wants you to minister so that you may go and do it.

Second, you must also realize that God may call you to do something that you would not necessarily choose to do. When God first called me to preach, I wanted to be an evangelist. But *"through many dangers, toils and snares,"* God revealed to me the call to become a pastor. I know of other examples in which a man has many *abilities,* but his *gift* is made evident when it is used in the way God called for it to be used. Such is the case with two very close friends of mine, Dr. Vince Massa who I've known for over 20 years and Dr. David Peacock who I've known for over 15 years. Both of these men know the Bible and they each have the ability to teach the Bible. But, if I were asked to comment on the calling of these two men, I would say that they are without question – pulpiteers. As a preacher observing them, I see that they have a unique ability to move the hearts of the people and draw lost souls to the foot of the cross. Both of them can do more than one thing, but the main gift that they possess is the ability to preach and deliver messages that effectively reach the hearts of those who come and listen to their preaching. So, as you ponder on the general call to preach, keep in mind that although many men are called to preach, we are not all called to minister the same way. We do not all possess the same unique abilities. There is no cookie cutter approach when it comes to the ministry. God uses each man in His own way.

Some preachers fail to understand that simple truth. Perhaps that is the reason why there are so many preachers out there who can't figure out what God wants them to do. Many times these men have a desire, but there is never a confirmation of their calling through some other avenue than desire. They concentrate on what God has done or is doing in some other preacher's life as the basis for making a decision about their own ministry. For example, I know of some preachers who mistakenly believe that since God called them to preach, then they must also be called to pastor. Such men can (and have) caused a lot of damage. They are like a five year old in an automobile. Yes, they are able to get behind the wheel, but all they end up doing is wrecking the car or killing someone. Don't be like a five year old. Don't wait until you see broken people and shattered lives all around you to realize God did not call you to pastor. Just because God called you to preach doesn't necessarily mean that He also called you to pastor.

Now there are those men that God calls specifically to pastor. And although they may be a great pastor, they could not be considered a great preacher. Nonetheless, God still called them to preach. In some cases, God calls a man to be an assistant pastor. An assistant pastor does not lead the flock, but he is called to help the primary man, which is the pastor. The assistant pastor helps in the church so that the pastor can get his work done. A bad situation can occur whenever the pastor leaves or dies and the assistant is left to take over the work. In many of these cases, the church dies under the leadership of the former assistant. This is simply because the man filling the position was not called to be the pastor, but to assist the pastor similar to the way Aaron and Hur lifted up the hands of Moses.

Maybe God has called you to teach in Sunday School or at a Bible Institute. Maybe God wants you to preach in the local church during those times when your pastor is out and he needs someone to fill in. Maybe God wants to use you in the nursing homes or in the jails and the prisons. The main thing is that God can use you. You, however, must realize that the gift God has given you must be used in the manner and in the ministry that He wants it used.

Now as far as evangelism is concerned, I believe that there are some men that God still calls to this ministry. However, there are a lot of fickle pastors out there that fall back on this ministry of evangelism. I'm talking about men who pastor for three or four years in a local church and then leave that church to answer the call to evangelism only to go out for a few years until they feel led to be a pastor once again. I don't believe in that kind of foolishness. Those types of individuals are usually looking for a way to get out of a situation or into a situation that fits them best. God has nothing to do with any of it. Be careful when it comes to that kind of thing.

There is the *taking* of a man, but it is your duty to find out what the task is that God wants you to do. When you find it, there will be a sense of joy and happiness in knowing that you are in the will of God.

The Making of a Man

A sculptor was once asked to make a statue of his king. All he was given was a block of stone. After he completed the great task, he presented it to the King, who then inquired, "How did you ever take that block of stone and transform it into my likeness." The sculptor replied, "Your majesty, I simply chipped away at everything that didn't look like you." And so it is with the Lord. However, it usually takes our lifetime for Him to perfect His will and way in us and transform us into His image.

God uses three ways to make a man. The first is by submission. In order for a man to lead, God must teach that man to follow. We have many bad leaders today in churches. Why? They never learned to follow. There are many men today who profess a call to preach. Many lay preachers can't wait for their pastor to go out of town in hopes that they might get a turn in the pulpit. They want to be the leader. They want to be the preacher, but they never learned how to follow. Listen, if God called you to preach, you'll find a pulpit. It may be a nursing home, a jail, or a street corner. You will find a pulpit somewhere. The first thing you need to learn is how to follow.

Consider the story of Elijah and Elisha in 1 Kings 19. In verses 19-21, we read about Elisha's call to the ministry. In that passage, there is nothing that indicates that Elijah had to persuade Elisha to follow. Elijah didn't try to encourage Elisha in any way. If you are ever going to be God's man, you better learn to follow God and submit yourself with or without any encouragement.

In verse 21, we learn that Elisha had a specific job to perform after he accepted his call to the ministry. His job was to minister to Elijah. He had to submit himself to another man. In 2 Kings 3:11, we read about Elisha again. Eight to ten years had passed since the time Elisha had first left everything to follow after Elijah. In the passage, Jehoram and Jehoshaphat were trying to get a word from the Lord, so they called on Elisha. But notice, in the years that had passed since Elisha entered the ministry, he had developed a reputation, not as being a great prophet, not as being a phenomenal miracle worker, but as being Elijah's servant. That was Elisha's reputation – a servant! He had been faithful as a servant in his ministry to Elijah. Gehazi could have had it, but he wasn't faithful (2 Kings 5:20-27). Many men miss out on the blessing of God upon their ministry simply because they do not recognize the importance of learning how to follow and they refuse to submit.

God's choosing of a man has nothing to do with seniority either. Seniority in the Lord doesn't mean a thing. I've learned that surrender, not seniority, is what matters to God. Now the Lord will reward you for serving Him a long time. But if a person is more surrendered than you, even if you have been saved longer, the Lord will bless that individual and use them. It's all about surrendering and submitting.

By their very nature, men do not like to submit. They don't like being under the authority of someone else. So they either resist or attack the authority of the one in charge. That was the same problem we read about in Isaiah 14 and Isaiah 28. Somebody didn't like somebody else being over them. It's the same way with human nature. Nobody likes the authority. But let me remind you, if you ever get to be the top boss, do you know what will still be over you? The book. Do you know what a lot of people (and preachers) do when they get to the height of where they want to be spiritually and everybody is looking up to them? They either forget the book or they try to rewrite it. Listen friend, we don't need to *rewrite* it – we need to *re-read* it.

Learn from Elisha's example. Submission is the key to success in the ministry. God never raises a man up to usurp the authority of the pastor of a local church. When a man does this, God is through with him as far as the ministry is concerned.

The second way God uses a man is through study. By studying the Bible, a man can **"shew himself approved unto God, a workman that needeth not to be ashamed, rightly dividing the word of truth"** (2 Timothy 2:15). A man who studies must give attendance to reading (that's what you're taking in), to exhortation (that's what you're giving out), and to doctrine (that's what you're learning) – 1 Timothy 4:13.

Many preachers never rise to the heights God wants them to nor do they reach their full potential. The reason why is plain and simple – they will not study. They refuse to be a student. They don't like to read, so they don't read. Then every time that they preach, you hear the same old song. If God has called you to preach, take time to study. Learn how to read and study. Practice on simplifying your sermon outlines and take the time to search out good illustrations for your messages. If you want to shine like a new dime in the pulpit, you'll have to read not only the Bible, but books, commentaries and other good material.

There is only one preacher that I ever met who only used the Bible. That was Bro. Lester Roloff. The rest of us will need to read. Bro. Roloff was different. He knew God in such a sweet way that he could just open up the book and preach. The problem is that most of us preachers don't know God that well. As I said earlier, the way God uses and works through one preacher does not mean that the same applies to every preacher.

I'll give you another example from a meeting in Florida years ago. The great North Carolina preacher, Dr. Carl T. Lackey was preaching in several services. There were a lot of Bible seminary students in attendance. One night Dr. Lackey opened up his sermon by saying something like this: "I don't need to pray before I begin, I'm ready to preach right now." One of the students there (I won't mention his name because he has become a good friend of mine and a good preacher over the years) was asked to preach during that meeting. As he began his message he said, "If Dr. Lackey doesn't have to pray neither do I." Well, about two minutes after he got started, God took that preacher's thoughts away. It wasn't long before he was on his knees begging the Lord to help him. What applied to Dr. Lackey obviously did not apply to that brother.

My point is this – we must be prepared before we step behind the pulpit; not only in our prayers, but also in our reading. There has to be reading and studying involved if you hope to become a good preacher. Personally, I try to read different books at the same time in order to broaden my thoughts. These include a devotional book for my own personal benefit, a theological book to keep sharp on my doctrine, as well as books about history and other topics. Then, when it comes time for me to preach, I can preach from a well of knowledge. By constantly feeding my mind with good information, I am not limited. I always have new and fresh material to draw from.

Your study should also involve listening to other sermons. Read and listen to all kind of sermons. There are also good

Christian newspapers to read, i.e., *The Bible Believer's Bulletin, The Flaming Torch, The Plains Baptist Challenger,* and *The Sword of the Lord* has some useful material in the sermons that they print. The key to remember is this. Read! Read! Read! Whenever we read, we enable ourselves to become better preachers for the people of our church and all who happen to hear us.

Now reading is not all that is required of us. Our preaching must also be endued with the Spirit of God. First and Second Samuel are great books to learn about the ministry in the Old Testament. In those days, the Holy Spirit came upon men and they were changed (1 Samuel 10:1-6, 9-10). Even Saul was given another heart. I know it's the Old Testament, but it's a great illustration.   Remember, Christians need to hear preachers that have been turned into another man, a man with a new heart. That leads us to the third step in God's process of molding a man into a preacher, which is the breaking of a man.

The Breaking of a Man

Spurgeon said, "God cannot use a man greatly until He has broken him greatly."[2] His observation lines up appropriately with scripture. For in Matthew 20:20-26, when James and John were looking for that special place beside the Lord, they were informed in verses 26-27 that the way up is down. The Bible makes it clear that if you want to be on top, you must go to the bottom. If you want to be first, you must be last. If you want to be chief, you must be a servant. That is the Bible way. And that is what is required if you are going to minister; **"but whosoever will be great among you, let him be your minister"** (Matthew 20:26).

The ministry is about service. If you are not willing to serve, then don't get into the ministry. Many people want to be ministered unto, but they by no means want to minister. I know that there are blessings involved with ministering, but many seek only the rewards while they shirk their duties as a servant.

To be great in the ministry, service to others is required. And to be chief, or number one, requires even greater service. There is a humbling that goes along with ministering and a greater responsibility that goes along with being chief (Matthew 21:28). The greatest servant of all gave His life for others, the Lord Jesus Christ. By His example, we know that the greatest of all services is to give your life for people, to lose yourself in the ministry itself. The ministry is not like any other occupation at all. Ministers must give their lives twenty-four hours a day and seven days a week.

The ministry will possess your heart and your thoughts. It will always be on your mind day in and day out. It will rob you of your time, possibly your life. The ministry requires you to die to yourself. There is no question about it.

I could spend pages telling you of the heart breaking stories in my ministry over the past twenty-nine years of preaching, nineteen of those as a pastor. From Dyersburg, Tennessee to Valdese, North Carolina there have been church splits and heartbreaks. People have tried to run me off. People have attacked not only me, but my family as well. They have physically hurt my son and they have lied about my wife. Some have put us through a fiery trial that felt as though it was Hell on earth. I've found that folks can hit me, cut me, or even shoot me, and I'll heal in a few weeks time. I might even have a scar to remember it by. But let me tell you, when they cut your heart, it doesn't heal too quickly. Those kind of cuts last a long time.

Early in my ministry God was breaking me to make me more effective as a preacher and a pastor. God called me to come to a place where there were twenty-two Baptist churches within a two square mile area. None of them were Bible believing works. So God had to toughen up my hide before He would let me come and minister. I believe that God did not want me to become just another wash-out Bible believing preacher. I'm referring to those preachers who set up their shingle and expect the multitudes to come. When they don't, they (the preacher) run off in search of greener pastures. God does not get any glory out of that.

As ministers, our duties require us to give our lives to the ministry. We are to serve others. You can't do that by yourself. You can't do it alone. It involves other people. Unfortunately, those who you minister to the most are the same ones that can cut your heart out the quickest. It has been said that Christians don't stab each other in the backs; they stab each other in the hearts. I have found that statement to be true from my own personal experiences.

I'm not complaining at all. In fact, looking back on it, I can now thank God for it all. Oh, the breaking is a blessing. It is how God gets a hold on your whole body, soul, and spirit. I have come to realize that it is only through this final step in God's process that He can transform the man, not only into the messenger, but also into the messenger that He wants that man to be.

3

The Preachers Heart

If there is anything wrong with today's church, it is the lack of preaching. I don't mean the failure to deliver a message, but the lack of common sense with regard to knowing how to preach. There is a lot of hot air blowing around today and a lot of volume. The problem is that Christians are spending more time listening to volume and looking at personalities than they are looking into what the Bible says. There's a lot of emotion, but there is no true heart. That's why this book will be different than most other books you will find on preaching.

In fact, what I am writing about in this book is probably against every Bible institute, every Christian college, and every seminary that you know of today. That's because they are not teaching men how to preach. These modern institutions are teaching people that three points and a poem are a message. That's not a message. A message comes out of the word of God. John R. Rice once said that his sermons had changed thousands of lives. I say that no man's sermon ever has or ever will change a life. Only the word of God changes lives. So, if you have been called to preach (as we discussed in the previous chapters), don't forget, it is not your abilities that God can use, it's you. God is not interested in your talents and abilities. God is interested in your heart. That's what I want to discuss briefly in this chapter.

The heart of a preacher is of key importance with regard to preaching. You see, preaching is not simply about writing sermons. I say that because God must make a man before He can ever make a message. We have discussed God's process for taking, making, and breaking. But, as a preacher, you must realize that all of that process depends upon your willingness to give your heart and your all to the Lord. Surrendering your heart to God comes first. It comes before developing your skills, techniques, and delivery. That's because God desires your heart. If you'll give God your heart, He can use you. Giving God your heart means that you are giving Him your all; everything that pertains to who you are – every facet of your life. Such a commitment demands inner strength and character. That's the only way that you will ever become an effective preacher.

If you are going to preach, you should want to be effective in your preaching. And preaching requires the whole man. Now if you are a business man, doctor, sports figure, lawyer, or any other professional, you can be good at what you do and still be lacking in a certain part of your character. There are many successful men in the secular world who have a defective character, yet they are great in their field of work. But this doesn't apply to successful preachers. If a preacher is going to be effective in the ministry, it requires the whole man, his body, his soul, and his spirit (1 Corinthians 9:27). This is where character plays a crucial role. Dr. J.R. Miller described the importance of character when he wrote:

> The true test of life is character. All else is extraneous, belonging to the husk, which shall fall off in the day of ripening; character is the kernel, the wheat, that which is true and enduring. Nothing is worthwhile save that which we can carry with us through death into eternity. The Apostle Paul puts it in a sentence when he says 'The things which are seen are temporal; but the things which

are not seen are eternal' (2 Corinthians 4:18). It is altogether possible that a man may fail of winning any earthly greatness, any distinction among men, anything that will immortalize him in this world's calendars, and yet be richly and nobly successful in moral things, in a ministry of usefulness, in things which shall abide when mountains have crumbled. It is possible for one to fall behind in the race for wealth, for honor, for distinction in art or literature, and yet all the while to be building up in himself a fabric of beauty and strength which angels shall admire.[1]

Strength of character from within has everlasting rewards. The Bible instructs us to **"look to ourselves, that we lose not those things which we have wrought, but that we receive a full reward"** (II John 8). To fight a good fight and finish the course requires exercising the inner man and it involves much discipline. However, strength of character from within is not the only area where preachers must apply discipline. A preacher must also have control over his body. This goes beyond resisting the temptations that might cause him to fall into sin. I'm talking about the necessity of taking care of the body. Many preachers have cut their ministry short because they simply failed to take care of themselves. They have over indulged and under-exercised their bodies.

As preachers, we must also learn to control our hearts (Proverbs 4:23). Let me assure you that if you fail to keep your heart, you'll be out of the ministry in no time. Don't worry about protecting and perfecting your talents more than your heart. Concentrate on preserving your heart towards the Lord Jesus Christ. How often do we hear of those preachers who have fallen out of the ministry because they didn't guard their hearts? These are preachers who get so busy and caught up in performing the work of the ministry that they fail to protect themselves. When sin comes by they fall into it (Acts 20:28).

If God has called you to the ministry, you will also need to have a heart for those you minister to. Your heart should set its affection on things above (Colossians 3:2) and your heart should also be devoted to the same things that Jesus loves on this earth, especially His church. Remember the passage where Jesus asked Peter if he loved Him? When Peter answered, **"thou knowest that I love thee"** (John 21:17), Jesus instructed him to **"feed my sheep."** In order to feed the flock, each of us, as pastors, must have a heart that not only loves the Lord Jesus Christ, but also the church that He died for. There is a responsibility that comes with that commitment. A closer examination of Acts 20:28 reveals some steps that preachers should follow as they fulfill the work of a minister.

God's Directive	The Preacher's Duty
Take heed therefore unto yourselves	Private Devotions
and to all the flock	Particular Duties
over the which the Holy Ghost hath made you overseers	Personal Calling (as overseer of the local church)
to feed the church of God	Public Ministry – (the work God has called you to)
which he hath purchased with his own blood.	Purchased Possession

An effective preacher will fulfill the aforementioned duties listed in this passage. These duties require each of us to maintain inner character, discipline, and a devoted heart. To accomplish the tasks successfully, the whole man is required; his body, his soul, and his spirit. And when I say spirit, I am also referring to his mind (Romans 12:2).

The greatest battlefield in the life of a Christian is located in the mind. It is where the actions of the body and the soul are controlled. As a preacher, you must protect your mind at all costs and keep a close watch over the gates of the eyes, ears, taste, smell, and touch. If a preacher is going to be effective, he must guard these entrances in order to maintain control of his thoughts, his emotions, and his will. Paul made special mention of the warfare that takes place in the mind (Romans 7:23). He explained this battle in more detail in 2 Corinthians 10:3-5 where he wrote:

> **3) For though we walk in the flesh, we do not war after the flesh:**
> **4) (for the weapons of our warfare are not carnal, but mighty through God to the pulling down of strongholds;)**
> **5) Casting down imaginations, and every high thing that exalteth itself against the knowledge of God, and bringing into captivity every thought to the obedience of Christ;**

In Ephesians 6:12-17 the Lord tells of our spiritual armor specifically designed for the battle and part of that armor is intended to protect your head. As a preacher, you wield the sword (Hebrews 4:12). But if you're going to use the sword, you had better be using your head. The helmet is not only for your salvation. In the context of the passage, it is also for your protection against "principalities, against powers, against the rulers of the darkness of this world, against spiritual wickedness in high places." All of those are listed as being "of this world." That means they are working in this world against you and against the cause of Jesus Christ. So, in order to be effective, a preacher must protect his mind from invasion. How can this be done? We find the answer given to us in Proverbs 23:26, which says:

> **My son, give me thine heart, and let thine eyes observe my ways.**

4

Preaching with Priorities

Whenever we set out to preach, our priorities must be right. If not, then our sermons and our messages won't be right either. The result will be that the people sitting under the preaching will suffer. They may suffer because we fail to study properly. They may suffer because we misapply doctrines. They may suffer because the scriptures are not presented in such a way as to adequately present the whole counsel of God rather than just a part of it. Even worse, they may suffer because our hearts are not in the right relationship with God. All of this can and will impact a preacher's message. If the Lord made every preacher listen to their sermons and hear it as their listeners do, I'm certain it would deflate a lot of ecclesiastical egos. I can assure you that each one would cry out like Cain, "Lord, the burden is much more than I can bear." Much of the problem stems from the fact that too many preachers do not have their priorities in line.

Now as I have stated, the first priority for you, the preacher, is to make sure that the Lord has your heart. A dedicated life with a heart devoted to God is a life worth living. Not only must our lives reflect the priority of Christ but our messages should also do the same. This applies both to what we preach and how we preach it.

A preacher must give his all if he expects to accomplish the goal of preaching in a biblically sound manner. You may be surprised to learn that this requires inserting an element of class when it comes to your preaching. In its simplest form, class is the appropriate application of tact. We should strive to be tactful whenever we prepare a message or stand in the pulpit to preach it. Unfortunately, there are many preachers who take great pride in standing before their congregations only to say, "Well ya'll, I'm just ignorant and unlearned, but at least I've been with Jesus." No doubt! We can surely tell that the first part of that confession is true. But what kind of ambassador would want to represent their King in such a fashion? This is where it is necessary to use a little class and a little tact. Developing this quality in your preaching must be a priority.

Now when I say class, I am not referring to money or riches. Class has nothing to do with how much money you have or the price of your suit. Class is the product of self-discipline and knowledge. It is a confidence attained by the preacher who has committed himself and proven that he can meet the ministry's challenges. Class also involves a degree of sacrifice. It is formed throughout God's process of calling a man, which we discussed in Chapter 1 and 2. Class is developed through God's process of taking, making, and breaking a man. But it also involves an effort on our part. None of us will be successful in preaching unless we give it everything we have. So don't become an ordinary preacher! There is a world full of them. Become something extraordinary. The way to do that is to take something ordinary and then elevate it to something *extra*ordinary. It is important to let people know what we stand for, but even better to let them know what we won't stand for. That is an essential part when it comes to instilling class into preaching.

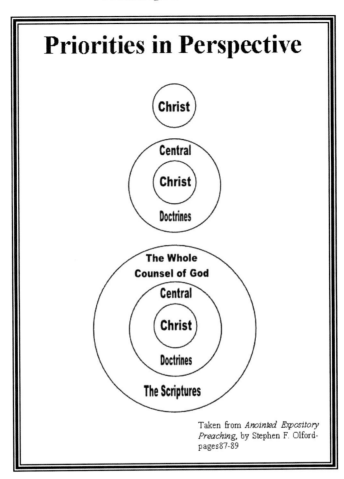

Priorities in Perspective

Christ

Central
Christ
Doctrines

The Whole
Counsel of God
Central
Christ
Doctrines
The Scriptures

Taken from *Anointed Expository Preaching*, by Stephen F. Olford- pages87-89

Christ – The First Priority

The very first thing we as preachers must center on is the Lord Jesus Christ. He is our message. He must always be the center of our message and our lives.

As Olford stated, "It is possible to preach messages based on biblical texts and still miss the central message."[1] But we must never fail to miss the central theme. Paul, the apostle to us Gentiles, reiterated the central theme of his sermons throughout the Pauline epistles:

Romans 1:16 – **For I am not ashamed of the <u>gospel of Christ</u>; for it is the power of God unto salvation to everyone that believeth; to the Jew first, and also to the Greek.**

1 Corinthians 1:18 – **For the <u>preaching of the cross</u> is to them that perish foolishness; but unto us who are saved it is the power of God.**

1 Corinthians 2:2 – **For I determined not to know anything among you, save <u>Jesus Christ, and him crucified</u>.**

2 Corinthians 5:19 – **To wit, that God was in Christ, reconciling the world unto himself, not imputing their trespasses unto them; and <u>hath committed unto us the word of reconciliation</u>.**

Colossians 1:28 – **Whom we preach, warning every man, and teaching every man in all wisdom; that <u>we may present every man perfect in Christ Jesus</u>.**

John 14:6 – **Jesus saith unto him, I am the way, the truth, and the life: no man cometh unto the Father, <u>but by me</u>.**

What do these verses tell us? They tell us that Jesus Christ is the power of God unto salvation. They tell us that the preaching of His cross is the power of God. They teach us not to know anything in our preaching, save Jesus Christ and Him crucified. They remind us that Jesus Christ hath committed unto us the word of reconciliation so that we may present every man perfect in Christ Jesus.

Preaching Jesus Christ is the only way our message will be effective. He is indeed our message. Therefore, to preach the truth we must consistently keep Christ as our main message and as our central theme. Why has truth fallen in the streets as Isaiah spoke of in Isaiah 59:14? It has happened because Jesus Christ no longer receives the preeminence in the message. The Lord said that if He was lifted up, He would draw all men unto him. When men and women are no longer drawn to Him it is because His truths have been removed from doctrines, from denominations, and even from the Bible. Preachers have allowed this to happen. They have failed in their responsibilities.

We are in a precarious position today in this Laodicean Church Age. It seems that many preachers know just enough Bible truth to make them armed and dangerous. They attach their errors to the truths of the word of God. Allow me to caution you. As preachers, whenever we decide to leave the truth of the Bible, we lose our only anchor. That is when we will start to drift towards the rocks of catastrophe and imminent destruction. That is when our sails will be blown by the turbulent gale force winds of apostasy and heresy. Christians and their churches die spiritually because they end up shipwrecked upon the rocks. This is often the result of preachers who fail to accept the responsibility that accompanies knowing the truth. Who can survive in such tempestuous seas?

Preachers and their churches must cry aloud for truth. They must hunger for it. It must be more than just a craving to hear or learn of something new like the Athenians did in Acts 17:21. It must be a hunger for real Bible truth. And if it happens to be a new truth, I can tell you this. New truth must come from old truth to be real truth. Once God has shown you the truths from that book – do not compromise.

When I say compromise, I'm talking about something much more serious and significant than compromising what you eat, what you wear, where you go, or what you watch. The danger lies with rejecting the factual and scriptural truths of the word of God – that is compromise.

That is why I believe that as a preacher, none of us can get too radical about truth in spite of what anyone says. The same holds true for any Christian. I take my hat off to those preachers who can stand for the truth in a bad crowd, but I have even more respect for those who refuse to get in with or run with the wrong crowd. Beware of trying to edge your way in with the popular crowd. I say that because I know from experience that you are not going to be what you decide to be. You are going to be what you decide to be around. That's where you'll step into a snare.

If you are going to keep the truth from falling, as a preacher, you must determine to make Jesus Christ the message that you bring. Since He is our Message, Christ must always be first place in our preparation, in our passions, and in our sermons.

Central Doctrines

Doctrine is the first application of the scriptures. In 2 Timothy 3:16, the Bible says that all scripture **"is profitable for doctrine, for reproof, for correction, for instruction in righteousness."** Doctrine is the foremost item on the list.

I have seen doctrines change in recent days. It is a sign of the latter times as men give heed to **"seducing spirits and *doctrines* of devils"** (2 Timothy 4:1). As a preacher, I have not been asked to respond. Instead, I have been raised to respond. As part of my response, I am required to do the following:

- **feed my flock and nourish them with good doctrine** (1 Timothy 4:6)
- **"give attendance to reading, exhortation, and doctrine"** (1 Timothy 4:13)
- **adorn my preaching with the doctrines of God our Saviour in all things** (Titus 2:10)

I am responsible for lifting up the central doctrines. They must also adorn the core message, which is Christ, and they must be preached.

The Whole Counsel of God

When it comes to preaching the whole counsel of God, no two preachers are alike. No two are the same. Unfortunately, this is where many preachers make a big mistake when it comes to starting and establishing a New Testament local church.

So many preachers try to make their new work look and operate like some other established church. They even chose the same name (or close to the same name) as some other church they admire. Don't let that be your priority.

The important thing to remember when you are building a new work or maintaining the work God has given you is this: Learn *how* to preach, *when* to preach, *what* to preach, and to *whom to preach it.* Then you will be able to preach the whole counsel of God.

Focusing on those things will help you to keep your priorities right when it comes to preaching. If you are a new preacher, starting a new local church, you won't have the same responsibilities as a veteran pastor. Don't let imitating some other work or preacher be your main motivation. Be thankful for the people God has given for you to preach to.

Let your main emphasis be upon Christ and a love for the truth. Truth is God-given – error is not. That is why keeping the biblical perspective is so critical.

Based on the last part of the priority chart, Olford quoting Sinclair Ferguson gives us some questions we should ask ourselves as preachers:

> Am I covering the whole range of biblical teaching – Old and New Testament, historical and theological, poetic and prose, exhortatory and denunciatory? Am I covering the whole range of biblical doctrines – God and man, Christ and Spirit, sin and grace, heaven and hell? Am I dealing with all the applications of the gospel message – to individual, home and family, business and pleasure, man and woman, church and society, personal and civil?[2]

5

Touching Human Needs

Now if there ever was a need in Christianity today, it is the need for preaching that can touch the needs of the hearers. Most preaching we hear these days is preached either to elevate the preacher or to show off his Bible knowledge and oratorical powers. Meanwhile, people in the pews are suffering spiritually because the messages fail to speak to the needs that people have in their lives.

As I have said, we preachers are called to preach an eternal message to eternal souls, which will have eternal repercussions. We must ensure that when we preach, people are touched. This is essential. It is one of the most, if not the most, important factors when it comes to preaching. Be ever mindful of this. Preachers think differently than church members. The preacher's or pastor's primary life is spent around studying the Bible and books about the Bible. He receives credit when things go well and has a tendency to shuck the blame off on someone or something else when things go bad. If people are not being ministered to through our preaching, then we have no one to blame but ourselves.

This means we must spend time in the book. Just as the apostles in Acts, we must give ourselves continually to prayer and to the ministry of the word (Acts 6:4). Like the apostles, we must set aside time for that specific purpose. That is the only way we can ever minister effectively. That is all part of our calling. In so doing, God can give us the messages that we need to address the needs of the people.

Many times the preacher/pastor may seem like he isn't a regular person, at least in the eyes of the congregation. That's mainly because he is regularly studying and thinking about theological matters and spiritual concerns. Conversely, the church members are thinking about life and the things of life (family, finances, work, health, kids, marriage, house payments, bills, etc.) and every thing else that pertains to earthly, physical matters. We cannot fail to remember that when we preach. We are preaching to real people who are dealing with real problems in their lives. Preachers who fail to remember this will end up overdriving their sheep by putting too many expectations upon them. This could cause them to die spiritually (Genesis 33:13).

Good preachers learn to think like the ones in the pew, especially when it comes to touching their human needs. We must all learn to empathize and sympathize with the problems that our congregations deal with on a daily basis. And remember that even though they may be faithful in their attendance, at times they'll be sitting there thinking about their own personal problems, regardless of how great the message is. There will be times when they might be watching you preach as they sit there in the pew, but they won't be able to concentrate and hear. Their own thoughts can drown out the voice of the preacher. I've learned that a person's mind and body can indeed be in two different worlds.

Your mind should still be focused on the message when you preach. There will be those times when you preach what you consider to be a great message, but based on the response you get, you'll begin to wonder. There will also be times when it will seem as though the audience doesn't really exist.

That's why you and I cannot judge a sermon by the response we get or by the congregation's involvement as evidenced by how many amens we hear. That is all superficial encouragement. There will be times when the preaching is a lot better than the people are letting you know. There may not be any amens at all, but God will be working in their hearts. That's why you must learn to bypass your own ego and doubts. Concentrate more on touching their human needs with a message from God.

Unless the preaching of Christianity works for the real person in the real world, it doesn't work at all. Many times you'll hear pastors preaching a message that really touches his members where they live. Then again, there are those times when it seems that the message belongs on Jupiter or some other planet, certainly not for anybody on the face of the Earth. This happens whenever the message fails to speak to and address the issues of the heart and it misses the people in the pews. We should never forget that there is a real world out there beyond the church building. The people want to know, and they need to hear, how to live the Christian life beyond the walls of the church house.

This requires a straightforward and practical application of the scriptures. Consider the four elements involved in accomplishing this task. 1) The preacher. He is the most important, for without him there is no one to preach the message. 2) The sermon. Without a sermon nothing would be said. 3) The scriptures. Without the scriptures there is no word from God. 4) The audience. Without the people, none of the other three elements would be necessary.

So whenever we stand in the pulpit to preach, it is our job to bring the theological concepts from the text in such a way that they address the needs of the audience. Preaching is always more effective when it is practical and personal. This aspect is as important as preparation and delivery.

Learn to preach so that you can speak to people where they live. Communicate with them. This involves speaking to an audience in their own vernacular. Choose your language appropriately. Once again, this can be different depending on the crowd you're called to minister to. Earlier I talked about the different backgrounds of God's men. Some can minister in places where others can't. It all depends upon their particular background. Being mindful of the audience's background is important if you want to gain their ear. That will help you to speak to them and communicate effectively.

But don't make the mistake of thinking that communication only involves what is said with the mouth. A preacher communicates with his life just as much as he does with his lips. In fact, a preacher can speak so loud with his life that no one can hear what he says with his mouth. That happens whenever he practices things in is life that don't match what he preaches from the pulpit. People have a word for preachers like that – *hypocrite*. We should make every effort to avoid that kind of communication. Learning to communicate appropriately involves not only our words, but our deeds as well.

With regard to the right manner of speech, we need to speak to people where they live. If your flock is country, then speak country, so that you can reach them. The same thing applies on the other side of the balance. Don't ever think it is a compromise to use proper English. However, be careful not to speak over people's heads with words they don't know and have never heard. Think about the Apostle Paul. His rudeness in speech never reflected an absence of knowledge (2 Cor. 11:6).

To touch human needs you will also need to be realistic. Keep your cool. Be careful in the things you say and do. Be watchful in all things, even your own preaching. Don't chase rabbits or entrap yourself with forgetfulness and carelessness.

These are important keys to success as a preacher. I realize that there are much better preachers than myself and that these men have much better outlines and messages than mine. But I also know that many of these same men have not learned to preach to people where they live. That is why you and I must think creatively so that we can have an impact on those who listen.

Brethren, we must keep in touch with the real world. Don't limit yourself to just understand the state of your own flock. Learn and study about human nature. Learn to recognize and understand the need element in people's lives. Jesus recognized the fact that people in this world are going to have troubles and problems. They have needs (John 16:33).

Nonetheless, every person has the moral and spiritual freedom to live either on the positive side or the negative side of biblical principles. In most cases, what a person does in response to the biblical principles will determine the results in their own personal experience. When you preach, be mindful of the fact that the majority of the people listening to you will be experiencing trouble. They will have a personal need. That means that they MUST HEAR FROM GOD. It is God's word that addresses a person's needs. God's words can satisfy man's spiritual needs the same way that food satisfies hunger, aspirin soothes a headache, and rest eliminates fatigue.

So with this realization in mind, ask yourself these questions before preaching a message:

- Why does anyone need to hear this message?
- What difference can this message make?
- Can it bring a deeper understanding of the text to the hearer?
- Can it make the hearer more conscience of God?
- Should I change my presentation of the message to reach people?

Remember that preaching needs to be both personal and practical, whereas teaching must be both theological and doctrinal. I did not say that preaching shouldn't be theological and doctrinal. I only want to emphasize the need to preach in such a way that the hearers can understand what is said and grab hold of it for help. We should make the message plain, simple, and easy to reach rather than force people to grab for the stars.   That is practical preaching. That is old path preaching.

When preaching is practical it will address the human need. It will offer a remedy to the main problem the listeners face. We all must remind ourselves that the fundamental remedy for every need is to trust God and have faith in Him. Faith is not ignited by the works of the hearers. Faith comes from calling attention to God; **"so then faith cometh by hearing, and hearing by the word of God"** (Romans 10:17).

The remedy for man's need is also conceptual. He suffers from being out of touch with God. Moreover, the remedy of man is volitional.   Man must choose to respond.   Our messages should encourage and persuade the listener to respond so that their most important human need will be met and satisfied, namely – fellowship with God through His Son, the Lord Jesus Christ.

6

Biblical Common Sense

One of the best North Carolina old path preachers ever born was Dr. Carl T. Lackey. Many years ago he gave me an important piece of advice concerning preaching. He said, "Red, God ain't in nothing that doesn't make common sense." At that time, I had no idea what he was talking about, but I do now. There's a reason why. When it comes to preaching, the message has to make common sense in order for it to reach the hearts of the folks that are listening.

The Apostle Paul recognized the importance of plain, easy to understand, "across-the-plate" preaching. In 2 Timothy 4:1-5, he gave Timothy the same kind of common sense instruction:

> **1) I charge thee therefore before God, and the Lord Jesus Christ, who shall judge the quick and the dead at his appearing and his kingdom;**
> **2) Preach the word; be instant in season, out of season; reprove, rebuke, exhort with all longsuffering and doctrine.**

3) For the time when they will not endure sound doctrine; but after their own lusts shall heap to themselves teachers, having itching ears;
4) And they shall turn away their ears from the truth, and shall be turned unto fables.
5) But watch thou in all things, endure afflictions, do the work of an evangelist, make full proof of thy ministry.

Paul even told the Ephesians in Chapter 6:19-20:

19) And for me, that utterance may be given unto me, that I may open my mouth boldly, to make known the mystery of the gospel, For which I am an ambassador in bonds: that therein I may speak boldly, as I ought to speak.

In both verses, Paul was simply giving us a common sense perspective as to what preaching is all about. Now back home, we used to say that *"something ain't what it ain't, and it sure ain't making it something that it ain't."* Think about that statement. You can't make anything into something that it's not. The same applies to preaching. Let's observe the verses in 2 Timothy 4:1-4 a little closer so that we can understand how to preach conscientiously, continuously, and comprehensively without disregarding basic common sense. When Jesus Christ preached, **"the common people heard him gladly"** (Mark 12:37). We should strive to do the same in our preaching. The following outline from Olford (*Expository Preaching*, p. 305-311) is a great encouragement to preachers:

Preaching Conscientiously

Paul's first instruction in these verses reminds us that the word of God must be preached conscientiously. In his instructions to Timothy, Paul immediately directs the young man's attention to God and to the Lord Jesus Christ. The charge here is both issued and received in their presence. We, too, must be ever conscientious of the charge we have received and also of the eternal accountability we have as preachers. Gentlemen, we are preaching for eternity! That is a serious matter. We are preaching from an eternal book that holds an eternal message that must be preached to eternal souls.

Notice verse one. Here, the warning gives reference to the Judgment Seat of Christ mentioned in 2 Corinthians 5:10. The application applies to the Church Age saint of God who has been quickened by the new birth (Ephesians 2:1-6), and it also has a reference to the Second Advent mentioning "his kingdom." Make no mistake. Preachers, we are all going to give an account of our preaching at the Judgment Seat of Christ.

10) For we must all appear before the judgment seat of Christ; that every one may receive the things done in his body, according to that he hath done, whether it be good or bad.

Don't overlook the seriousness of this passage. Always be conscious of this coming day. There are five things I want to bring to your attention about what this verse says. The first is the fact that there will be <u>perfect attendance</u> on that day, for the Bible says, "we must all appear." Second, there will be <u>personal accountability</u> for "the things done in the body." Not for what some other preacher did, but for what you did or did not do. That brings us to the third point: <u>painful acknowledgements</u> because the judgment will assess the value of your work. The verse here states, "according to that he hath done." Fourth, we find <u>precious rewards.</u> These will depend on those things done in our body, **"whether it be good or bad."** How will our works be tried? 1 Corinthians 3:13-15 tells us that they are going to be tried by <u>FIRE</u>.

13) Every man's work shall be made manifest: for the day shall declare it, because it shall be revealed by fire; and the fire shall try every man's work of what sort it is.
14) If any man's work abide which he hath built thereupon, he shall receive a reward.
15) If any man's work shall be burned, he shall suffer loss: but he himself shall be saved; yet so as by fire.

Preacher, there are many passages in which Paul expounds his thoughts concerning the rewards of the believer. The whole concept of eternal rewards is based upon eternal responsibilities. In order to preach responsibly, you must keep eternity in mind and not the things of this world. So whenever I preach my rule is this: No friends, no family, no foes, no finances.

Let me also throw in a word of caution at this point. If you have studied and prayed about the message and you know in your heart that you did your best in delivering the message, then leave the rest up to God. If you don't remember to do that, you will begin to question every sermon you preach. You must leave the results of your preaching up to God. If not, you'll eventually end up with ulcers and nerve problems. Ultimately, you will begin to doubt and question your calling. I learned a long time ago not to preach for a response. I preach for one reason and for one reason only. God has called me to preach. Woe is me if I if I don't. J. Frank Norris said, "First thoughts in order are from headquarters, everything else is human reasoning."[1] That's a good point to remember. Never let your human reasoning get in the way of your calling.

Continuing on with Paul's instructions to Timothy, we find more common sense applications about biblical old path preaching and what it is. Notice that in 2 Timothy 4:2 Paul said to **"preach the word."** Now in order to preach the word of God, you must have the word of God. If you don't have it, you can't preach it. That's just plain old common sense.

A preacher must be conscious and aware of the fact that there is a growth process associated with preaching. The only way you will grow as a preacher is to apply the principles that Paul lays out in these verses. First of all he says to reprove. To reprove is to convince someone of something that they are doing wrong. That is a reproof. It's like telling your child not to do something because it is wrong. Then there is a rebuke, which means to scold sharply, or to reprimand. This is where you lay the weight on in your preaching. Next is the instruction to exhort, which means to stir up. You are to exhort them with all longsuffering and doctrine. You can exhort people by preaching on the Second Coming or the Virgin Birth. The intent here is to encourage and build up people.

You will notice the progression of growth here in the life of a preacher. The first is when you can reprove. This is like grade school. This is when you first convince people that you can preach. That means you can reprove them. If you can never reprove anybody, then you'll never preach. That's part of what preaching is. Then there is the rebuking. That's like middle school. Here, you have grown a bit and you're a little older and a little smarter. You know a little better about when to apply the whip. You know right when to make the cut and when to hold off. The best way to cut somebody is when you've got them laughing or after they have just said a hardy amen. That's when you can throw a one-liner in there and crack'em. That's when it sticks in awful far. You can shove the sword in there a long way if you do it right. There's nothing wrong with turning your back on the crowd. Just say something thought provoking before you do. Then turn around and give them a few seconds to think about what you just said.

It's a lot like a bullfight. The greatest thing in the bullfight is when the matador gets the bull riled up in frenzy. Then he takes his cape, flings it around himself, and turns his back to the bull. All the attention becomes focused on what he just did, which was to turn his back on a wild bull. That captivates the audience. Then, when the bull comes around again, the matador can stick him just in the knick of time with his sword.

We can apply this illustration to preaching. The same concept will apply. It has to do with timing, which we will cover in more detail later on. Get the people going. Get them shouting amen and laughing. That's when you can stick them, turn around, and walk back to the pulpit. That will capture their attention and cause them to think about what was just said. When they come back around again, you can prick their hearts with the sword of the spirit, the Bible. The intent of these tactics is not to be arrogant or showy, but to help get the message deep down into the hearts of the people.

So the progression through the preacher's school of growth follows a pattern:

> **Reprove:**
> Grade school – to convince someone of something.
> **Rebuke:**
> Middle school – to lay the weight on someone.
> **Exhort:**
> High School – to stir up someone.
> **Longsuffering & Doctrine:**
> Post-graduate school – correctly applying the substance of biblical truths.

Notice also that in the first five verses of 2 Timothy 4, the word doctrine is repeated twice. What is so important about doctrine? Good doctrine makes for good preaching. False doctrine only leads to false preaching. I'm not talking about delivery here. It has nothing to do with the delivery. The fact is that you cannot feed sheep with goat's food. If you do, it won't be too long before they start butting each other and you.

Many Christians today have turned from sound doctrine. They have failed to realize the importance of sound doctrine in the proclamation of the gospel. Many people don't know what salvation really is because the preacher they listen to does not have the right doctrine to begin with. Preaching is part of biblically sound doctrine **"and how shall they hear without a**

preacher?" (Romans 10:14). When people throw out doctrine, they don't want to hear preaching, they want teachers. Always be conscious of whether or not your message is doctrinally sound.

Notice verses three and four in 2 Timothy 4. Now many preachers who have turned from **"sound doctrine"** have started a university, a Bible college or an institute. Today we are living in a time when men have heaped unto themselves teachers **"having itching ears."** It is a time of teachers not preachers.

You can follow this downward progression of the Church Age by examining Ephesians 4:11. At different times in the Church Age, there have been apostles, prophets, evangelists, preachers, and teachers. We know that the apostles and prophets ended in Acts 28. Next, there were evangelists. In America, we had evangelists from about 1750-1950. Around the 1920's and 1930's, there were two great evangelists, Billy Sunday in the North and Mordecai Ham in the South. One day Mordecai Ham preached in Charlotte, NC and a young man responded to the invitation and got saved. It was Billy Graham. He became the last real evangelist this country knew of before he slipped off into apostasy.

Then we come to pastors. These are found as we near the end of the verse. The spiral continues downward. Pastors do all kinds of things, including feeding the flock and the work of an evangelist. Notice, however, that the closer we get to the end of the age, the more the people want to learn. And just before the coming of Christ, we have an emphasis on teachers promoting teaching and learning. Turn on any television or radio and listen. You won't find many doing much evangelistic preaching. You'll rarely hear a pastor on the airwaves doing any kind of hard preaching against sin. What they are doing is teaching.

In the last part of the Church Age, the problem is teachers turning people away from the truth. That is exactly what we read in 2 Timothy 4:4. And that is what Paul warned Timothy about. These teachers turn the truth into fables, which are man-made stories with man-made ideas. So Paul reminded Timothy to be conscious of these things.

Young men today have a tendency to think that war is all glory, but that's not true. William Tecumseh Sherman said, "War is hell." When you are preaching, be conscious of the fact that you are in a spiritual battle for the souls of men. Preaching isn't all about getting up on the platform, hearing the amens, and getting the glory and attention for being a great pulpiteer. If that is the only reason you do it, you are not called to preach. You are doing nothing more than promoting yourself. Remember the center of the chart on priorities in Chapter 4. Who was found at the center of that chart? It wasn't a preacher. It was Christ.

Preachers are called to be a voice crying in the wilderness making a way for the Lord. Be conscientious of that fact. Our mission is to call the world's attention to the Saviour. Preach conscientiously; always keeping in mind the one that you preach for as well as what you are preaching about.

Preach Continuously

Paul said in 2 Timothy 4:2 that a preacher should preach the word continuously, **"to be instant in season and out of season."**

Chrysostom put it in other terms when he said, "Take opportunities and make opportunities."[2] If you are going to preach continuously, you must not let anything stop you. You will need to be always ready.

I hardly go to any meeting nowadays where I am not on the schedule to preach, but occasionally I'll go if there is someone I want to hear preach. When I go, I'm always sure to bring a message with me. I've seen many preachers get called on to preach unexpectedly at a meeting they were attending. There have been a few occasions when I've seen preachers reluctantly admit that they didn't bring anything to preach. They had to apologize for not having a prepared message with them. Don't let that happen to you. A preacher should always be prepared whenever he is called upon to deliver a message. If we can't do it from our notes, we should certainly be able to do it from our heart. Be ready to preach at any time and in any place.

Now this may sound strange to some of you, but every opportunity to preach is not necessarily an open door. Some preachers may try to encourage a young preacher by saying, "Next time you're around, let me know I'll have you preach for us." They say that out of the kindness of their heart, but that is not how it is taken. Instead, some young, inexperienced preacher will start planning on an evangelistic meeting, expecting to be treated and paid like the "Big Guns." Listen, gentlemen, I am here to tell you that things don't happen that way! You may have to learn the hard way, but take it from me that every opportunity is not an open door.

The main thing to focus on is learning how to preach both in season and out of season. It is a continuous call. You don't take a break from it. This is where the gift comes in.

God has given you a gift. It is a gift of preaching, that's what we're talking about here. The gift to preach is a God given gift. This gift is not taken away from the man to whom it is given. This gift will carry you through the in seasons and the out seasons of your ministry. Now you may not understand this, but what I'm about to say is true.

Many preachers in the past few years have fallen to sin, yet, they were preaching undetected by the body of Christ before their sin was ever found out. Before they were ever exposed in their sin, they were preaching and folks were getting saved and responding to their messages in other ways. God didn't take away the gift and God also blessed His word. As far as the message was concerned, it didn't matter whether or not the vessel was a clean vessel or a dirty vessel. The word of God did not return void. And God did not take away the gift that he gave to the man. What I am saying is that **"the gifts and the calling of God are without repentance"** (Romans 11:29).

I'm not saying these things to give you an open door to go off and start sinning as a preacher. Preachers are required to have a high standard of character, morals, and chivalry. If you are a preacher, then your standards ought to be higher than those of your congregation. As the old saying goes, "the pew will never rise higher than the pulpit."

All of us reap what we sow. Eventually, things come out in the open. Even though through repentance God will forgive a fallen preacher, many of the saints simply will not.

Once you've crossed over that line, God may still use you again. That's true. But it's probably going to be a real dull crowd you're preaching to, especially if they would tolerate a preacher whose sin has been exposed.

I know that these things can happen. It used to drive me up a wall to hear about preachers who had sinned, especially when I realized that they were having some illicit affair during the same time they were preaching meetings. I have even listened to some of them preach while their "exploits" were still going on and they seemed to be right on with the message. I used to think it was because the flesh and the spirit are so closely alike that only the Bible could see the difference.

But I don't think that anymore. Instead, I believe that God doesn't take the gift away, but He does take way the unction. It reminds me of the old illustration about the preacher who arrived late to his church one Sunday evening. As he approached the door to the church, he could hear people weeping and wailing throughout the congregation. The preacher flung open the doors and looked to the pulpit only to find that it was Lucifer himself preaching a sermon about Hell. The stunned preacher ran up to the pulpit and asked, "How can you preach about hell and get this kind of response?" The Devil replied, "It's easy. Anyone can preach truth without unction." How true!

So if we are going to preach in season and out of season, we must remember that God will bless his gift in spite of our sin. That's no justification for sin. Nonetheless, we must all watch ourselves closely and stay confessed up.

Paul instructed Timothy to watch in verse 5, **"watch thou in all things."** If you are going to continue in the ministry, you will also need to watch out for the twins of sin – money and morals. If a man's money is wrong, his morals will follow. If his morals are wrong his money will follow. Many preachers have this problem. Believe me when I say that these men were through in the ministry long before they ever left.

As a preacher, be careful not to be influenced by changing times or clashing trends. Continue on the old path. This warning is alluded to in verses three and four of 2 Timothy 4. As a preacher, don't preach what itching ears want to hear. This problem isn't just found in modernistic churches. It occurs in Bible believing churches as well. It will happen when you start swinging from one extreme to the other on the theological pendulum. It includes everything from **"touch not; taste not; handle not"** (Colossians 2:21) to those dry-eyed theological messages that will not make the heart soft to the Holy Spirit. Those kinds of messages serve no useful purpose when it comes to effective ministry.

Also watch out for those messages that are aimed more at the head than the heart. Such messages are easy to preach because they don't ever trouble the conscious of the hearer. Such messages are not from God. They come from the hearts of men who wish to control their congregation. Many folks will kick the Southern Baptist Convention because of the control they wield over their churches. I suggest that we, as Bible believers, stop and take a good long look at ourselves. It won't take long to see the same kind of bishops, cardinals, and popes right in our own backyard. In spite of all that kind of foolishness and the fact that people are turning away from the truth of God unto the fables of men, our mandate remains the same and we must continue in it…preach the word!

Over the years I have had the blessing to visit Washington, D.C. I've seen the great memorials dedicated to this nation's Armed Forces. I've seen Arlington Cemetery, the Tomb of the Unknown Soldier, and the Vietnam Memorial: "the Wall." They are very impressive monuments. However, back in

1968, I saw a war memorial unlike all the rest. It has never left my mind even though it has been some 35 years ago.

I was a young Marine at Khe-Sanh firebase. There I saw a line of weapons stuck barrel down into that sandy earth. Helmets hung on the rifle butts along with a set of dog tags dangling underneath. Each rifle stuck into that war torn battlefield represented a Marine who had lost his life in the fight. I believe that was the greatest memorial my mortal eyes will ever see.

Gentlemen, just as those men laid down their lives and gave their all in the line of duty, we too, as good soldiers of Jesus Christ, should never fail to preach the word. We should preach it continuously; regardless of whether we are in a pastorate, a Sunday school, on a street corner, or on a foreign field as an evangelistic missionary. Until we draw our last breath, we should continually be telling the old, old story of Jesus and His Love.

Preach Comprehensively

To preach the word comprehensively simply means to preach the whole council of God. Preach it so that it can be understood every time. Preaching must convict those who hear it. People must be brought to a place where they realize their sinful state. This approach will bring about true repentance. In fact, that's the only way repentance will occur as a result of preaching.

Second, preaching must correct those who have erred and then communicate what God requires to make things right.

Third, preaching should build-up and encourage as we **"exhort with all longsuffering and doctrine."** That's why I am an expository preacher. Expository preaching constructs a solid foundation with truths taken directly from the Bible. Those truths are strong, powerful, and from the throne of God. They will not give way when people build their lives upon them. Expository preaching also feeds the soul and touches the heart.

In my own personal opinion, other styles of preaching only serve to delight the mind and feelings. Or in some cases, insult the hearers with sarcasm and rudeness. We should not be interested in the Nicolaitan approach to preaching that only leads to preacher worship. We have no need for applause or the accolades of men. What we do need is God's power.

Expository preaching is a main characteristic of old path preaching. It's focus is on the Bible. It amplifies a resounding **"thus saith the Lord."** An exposition of the text will reveal your own inadequacies and weaknesses, but it accentuates the power of God's word (Hebrews 4:12).

Preach Courageously

Preaching must be courageous. You will be forced to stand in the face of the world and denounce sin. The response of men will not always be favorable. Afflictions will come, but you must find the courage it takes to stand in afflictions. Paul instructed Timothy to watch in verse five of 2 Timothy 4. Watch for afflictions. Don't worry. If you are preaching the way you are supposed to and doing the things God called you to do, you won't have to watch very long before afflictions come. You will not have to invite them. They will come on their own (John 16:1-3, 1 Peter 4:12).

As preachers, we must endeavor to live our lives in that manner. In order to do so, we must possess the courage to endure grave afflictions. But don't be foolish. Self-inflicted wounds are difficult to care for and they certainly aren't an indication of spiritual bravado. Let me explain.

Years ago, when we were first starting out, Bro. Vince Massa, Bro. David Peacock, and I all had quite a reputation following us. I suppose that you could say we were the three burrs under the saddles of a lot of established preachers who thought that they were the theological experts of their day. Many times these preachers would come up and remind us that we needed to cool it down a little when we preached.

Over the years, I ended up building a reputation as a hard preacher. Even today, at 55 years of age, that reputation still follows me. I detest that. That's because I'm not a hard preacher. I'm just a biblical preacher. What I'm saying is this: Gentlemen, we must watch the way that we dispense the truth. The truth will cost you something. Don't prematurely sign on the dotted line if you're not willing to take up the mortgage payments. In our preaching, it is not enough to just preach the gospel. Yes, we must preach the truth and judgment as well. But our preaching must not only be our voice. Our preaching must be our voice coupled with God's word in order to get men to embrace it.

7

Skill, Development, Discipline & Goals

Skill

When speaking of skill, the first thing a preacher should keep in mind is that skill does not refer merely to your style and delivery, but also to the collection, choice, and arrangement of materials. Skill refers to an ability to construct a sermon so that it can be used effectively. This kind of skill is gained by years of training and experience. Once a preacher has learned how to select and construct the sermon message that God has laid on his heart, he must then learn how to make the message persuade the hearers. Effective preachers must also be persuasive speakers. Whenever such a man is found, scarcely and without exception, this man will be found to have labored much in order to acquire his skill.[1] Why? Because skill involves practice. It is only through much practice that the characteristics of good preaching can spring forth. What are the characteristics of good preaching? Preaching should be apt, apparent, full of true feeling, fearless in rebuking sin, and so addressed to the heart as to enlighten the spirit and subdue the will.[2]

Second, preaching must be more than an outlines and a delivery. It must be something divine. It must consist of a Divine calling with a message that penetrates the flesh and burrows down into the soul. Such preaching convicts the hearers of their sin, mends misery, sorrows, burdens, and gives light where the weary souls can find rest, comfort, and peace. This is old path preaching. It is real preaching. Real preaching occurs only when the Divine moves upon the deliverer. How can we describe real preaching?

It is the thundering of the fists joining with the lightning strike of the points to embed the message into the hearts of the congregation. It is the unction, power, and wisdom from on high mixed with plain and simple down-home country sense. Such preaching is just and holy. It is divine. It is a supernatural transaction where the book of God and the vessel of God become one. It is the voice of one crying in the wilderness. In that moment, the congregation becomes blurred, faces become unknown, and the speaker becomes a holy vessel for God's anointing oil. When God gets in the message, there is unction, power, sweat, and the body feels as if sparks are flying off the finger tips with every "thus saith the Lord." Saints rejoice with the enlightened word of God as the Lord Jesus Christ is lifted up, exalted, and magnified. Such preaching melts away the evil like a hot cathead biscuit melts away farm fresh butter. Real preaching is lifting up the One that the message is about, the Lord Jesus Christ. Nothing more. The message should always be more important than the messenger. Yes, man calls preaching foolishness, but God is pleased with the right kind of preaching.

Development

With regard to developing skill, I am reminded of the time that I took my son to watch the Chicago Bulls play the Charlotte Hornets. It was an exciting experience to watch the pros. They were all good players. But one player stood out among the rest – Michael Jordan. We watched as he maneuvered the court, positioned himself in the key, and slam-dunked the ball over the other players. He seemed to be unstoppable. He rebounded. He assisted. He scored. That night we watched a master at basketball. I remember telling my son. "I wish I could do that." But you know, for me, that was only a dream; because what my son and I watched was more than the just a man playing basketball. We watched a gifted player applying years of practice, training, studying, sweating, and conditioning. That night it all came together and resulted in an outstanding performance.

I could never become a master of basketball like Michael Jordan regardless of how much I loved the sport or how badly I wanted to become great at it. But, I learned something that night in Charlotte, NC. I realized that I had to choose something that I could be good at doing. And realizing that I could only be good at a few things in my life, my choice was none other than preaching. But preaching is different than any other profession. The difference is that we cannot play at preaching for we are preaching for an eternity. That was Spurgeon's viewpoint (the great Prince of Preachers). He also made it clear that our profession – preaching – is the most important of all vocations. Why? It's because life, death, hell, and worlds unknown may hang on the preaching and hearing of a sermon. Therefore, in order to excel, you and I must continue to develop our preaching skills and recognize the key components that are required if a man is going to preach and preach well.

1. Skill: The proficiency or expertise in a particular craft gained by   training and experience.
2. Development: The gradual growth that occurs over time through practice, thereby causing skills to become fuller, larger, and better.

The combination of points one and two above result in the third and final component:

3. <u>Skills development:</u>   This is the gradual growth of ones proficiency in a particular craft. Skills are developed through step-by-step training. The training requires patience. With regard to preaching, skills development is usually limited to delivery.

With that being said, we now can focus our attention on six things that the preacher must remember concerning his gift, or skills:

1. <u>Understanding</u>:   It   is   important   to understand the basic concepts behind the skills you are learning. If you understand what you are doing, it is more likely that you will remember how to do it.
2. <u>Experience</u>:   Hands   on   experience   is essential. You will never develop your skills in any work unless you are a doer not just a hearer.
3. <u>Trial and error</u>: Your skills are best learned step by step through trial and error.
4. <u>Every man is different</u>: Remember that neither men, nor preachers, are all alike. We   all   have   different   experiences, backgrounds, and skills.
5. <u>Study</u>.   Preachers   should   study   other preachers in order to learn. Watching other preachers preach will help you to visualize not only what to do, but also what NOT to do.
6. <u>Practice</u>: You have heard it said before and it bears repeating. There is no substitute for practice.   Even the greatest of the great

must practice. As the world-renowned pianist Leonard Bernstein once stated:

> When I go one day without practicing, I notice it. When I go two days without practicing, my family and friends notice it. And when I go three days without practicing, the whole world knows it.

There is only one way to become good at anything you set out to do - you must practice. And remember that practice doesn't make perfect, it does make permanent. So practice correctly.

I also like to think of what James Jamerson said years ago. He wasn't a preacher. He was a well-known studio musician back during the 1970s. Talking about music, Jamerson said, "If you can't feel it, then you can't play it." When you think about it, that's an astute observation. I say, "If you can't feel it, you shouldn't try to preach it."

Discipline

Preaching is an academic discipline. It calls for serious study. Never try to prepare for a preaching engagement for over three to four hours at a time. The mind and body will become weary, mentally fatigued, and frustration will set in. Charles Spurgeon said, "I scarcely ever prepare for my pulpit with pleasure. Study for the pulpit is to me the most irksome work upon this earth."[3] Have you found this to be true? If you have ever set out to prepare a sermon, you know that Bro. Spurgeon was simply being honest. Honest preachers will tell you that they are committed to good preaching. However, only a few are ever satisfied with their own sermon preparation or its results.

If the message is going to be successful, the preacher must approach the task at hand with passion. Remember that passion is the trigger for success. Whenever I get to a low point, I often ask myself, "Why am I doing this?" When it is all said and done, it comes down to passion. Success in the ministry is not the result of spontaneous combustion. You must set yourself on fire first. You must be passionate about not only what you are doing, but this, "Who you are doing it for?" That is where passion must combine with discipline. That is what we are trying to teach our students here at the Blue Ridge Bible Institute.

Beware of being a shoddy, undisciplined preacher. Preaching takes work and the work is hard work, especially if you are going to become a great preacher. If God permitted any of us to have success without hard work then we would become intoxicated with vanity. The study is hard, the preparation is hard, and the critique can be hard. Do you know what it means to preach and to preach well? Bob Jones Sr. gave these following tips on preaching, which I have tried to use over the years of my ministry.

- Question their intellect if they refuse to agree on what God said.
- Ridicule their character if they refuse to listen.
- Captivate their minds with common sense.
- Learn how to master the articulation of your voice.
- Master the use of southern or northern language; down home, everyday sayings.
- Learn and master the use of timing (and I would also add climate to this list).[4]

If a young man could learn these six things about preaching, it would pay off deeply in the way of success. The success I'm talking about here is not always seen in this life. The success I'm referring to is the success that a man leaves behind when he is gone. It is my desire to leave behind biblical preachers for the generations to come if Jesus tarries.

Brethren, you and I are not self-sufficient. We need help. We need God's help and we need each other's help if we are going to succeed as preachers. As we work together to become better preachers, we will take on an adventure of growth and development. But allow me to reiterate, it takes work. As I mentioned earlier, I've been preaching now for twenty-nine years, and I am still working on it. I still have to practice. I still have to apply myself. And I still have to discipline myself. The work of preaching is too important to neglect and too complex to take for granted.

Goals

It has been said that there are four steps to achievement: 1) plan purposefully, 2) prepare prayerfully, 3) proceed positively, and 4) pursue persistently. This requires establishing goals. In our pursuit to become good preachers, we can only achieve this objective by establishing *definite* goals. Otherwise, we end up aiming at nothing. There are goals when it comes to learning how to preach.

One of the goals you must set for yourself is to learn. A preacher must be always willing to read, study, and learn. Only through learning can we attain knowledge, values, and skill. There are three basic reasons for learning. Learn to expand your knowledge. Learn to increase your value. Learn to improve your skills.

Knowledge results simply from what is being studied. There are three things that must be studied to obtain knowledge of preaching.

1. Homiletics – deals with the preparation of preaching.
2. Hermeneutics – the subject that deals with literary interpretation.
3. Speech communication – this subject deals with getting your message across.

Values are your convictions. However, be sure that when you preach, you preach the word, not your convictions. This has become a malady in our time. In fact, it has been killing local churches with falsehoods for the past forty years. It has been said that if you don't preach your convictions you're not worth your salt as a preacher. I agree, but only if your so-called convictions are Bible based, not just founded on your own ideas or pet preaching points. Remember, we cannot legislate spirituality. No one wants to hear your list of rules and regulations.

Skills must be viewed in light of the differences we all possess. We are not all equal in intelligence or quickness of wit. Not all of us possess a sparkling dynamic personality. We are emotionally different as well. Some preachers are more passionate than others. Some are more caring. And some are fierier by nature. Some can speak exceptionally well and it is in their nature to clearly articulate what they are trying to say, while others seem to mumble or stutter. Some are naturally dramatic and extroverted and seem to relish the spotlight, while others churn with dread at standing before a crowd. When looking at biblical examples of preachers, we see all kinds of preachers from different backgrounds (i.e., farmers, shepherds, princes, soldiers, and fisherman). They were all different types of men who possessed different backgrounds, skills, abilities, and personality traits.

The New Testament discussion of spiritual gifts includes preaching as a distinct endowment from God and given by the Holy Spirit (1 Corinthians12:10, 28-29). A talent is a gift committed to ones trust to use and improve. Remember that the package of inherited traits is what you and I have to work with as we try to become the best preachers possible for God Almighty.

It has been my observation that many (let's say most) preachers know the rules of preaching, but unfortunately, they just don't know how to preach. One-hundred and twenty years ago, John Brodus wrote that a preacher needs:

> the capacity for clear thinking, with strong feelings, and a vigorous imagination, a capacity for expression, and the power of forcible utterance.[5]

Although you are not yet fully developed, you do have the gifts and skills that will be necessary for preaching, that is if you are truly called to preach. For the time being, you are a jewel in the rough. The sharpening and maximizing of your gifts and skills will be tried and prepared over time. As you begin to learn more about preaching and all that is involved, it is important that you keep the following thoughts in mind with regard to biblical preaching:

- Sermon preparation is a supernatural endeavor.
- Biblical preaching is not a mystery talent for only the most gifted.
- Anyone can learn the right methods to prepare for good preaching.
- Preaching is an art that calls for discipline before freedom.
- Old habits will resist biblical methods of discipline.
- Preaching is something that clarifies biblical ideas with word crafting (i.e. – the ability to find the right words to express the passage).
- The Bible (KJV) is an unlimited source for fresh, timely preaching.

In the next chapter, we will look at one of the most fundamental skills pertaining to old path preaching – the proper approach to view the text and preparing the sermon outline.

8

The Text in View

It is always important to keep the biblical text within view. In order to accomplish this task, a preacher must allow the listeners to continually observe or see what the Bible is saying. This requires observation. Observation is the art of reading the text and applying the correct and appropriate biblical view. In order to achieve this objective, the preacher has two distinct methods at his disposal: 1) the *inductive* method, and 2) the *deductive* method. After choosing the right approach, there are other important factors that must be considered as part of the sermon preparation process.

Inductive Method

The inductive method looks at the particular facts within a passage in order to establish a general conclusion about what is stated and what the text actually means. It is a process that both begins and ends with the scriptures. Make no mistake about it, the inductive method requires work and it is typically a very labor-intensive approach to sermon preparation. It also demands discipline, diligence, concentration, and meditation.

Concentration and meditation are never easy when it comes to preparing a biblically sound sermon. It is a mentally taxing activity. That is where discipline and diligence play a vital role. As Alfred P. Gibbs points out in his book *The Preacher and His Preaching*, concentration and meditation are both absolutely essential in order to properly prepare and write a message. Gibbs illustrates this point with a quote from an author named Stephen Leacock, who was once asked about his formula for successful writing. Leacock replied, "All you have to do is to procure pen, paper, and ink, and then sit down and write as it occurs to you." Then he added, "The writing is not hard, but the occurring: that, my friend is the difficulty."[1] This same truth can be applied toward preaching. Albeit, our job as a preacher demands that we **"labour in the word and doctrine"** (I Timothy 5:17). That is the job that we must prepare and train ourselves to do.

The inductive method is preferred because it allows the scriptures to speak for themselves. Using this approach, a preacher can prepare a message by applying the principles found in Isaiah 28:10; placing **"precept upon precept, line upon line, line upon line; here a little, and there a little."** Within the context of that passage, we also find in Isaiah 28:9 that this is God's chosen design for communicating doctrine to the hearers. Applying yourself to the inductive method is never an easy task; however, it allows the Bible to speak for itself as "thus saith the Lord." Furthermore, it is the safest way to avoid the dangerous pit that many preachers fall into when they end up using the scriptures to preach their own private interpretation and convictions.

Only a few Bible believing preachers and pastors these days realize that the inductive approach is the best approach for getting the text in proper view. It simply means that you come to your text and examine it as thoroughly as possible. This method is required if a preacher is to obtain a full understanding and true meaning of the passage. Keep in mind that the Bible was given to us in order to reveal God, not to hide Him. Therefore, the inductive method should be the preacher's first choice for expounding the Bible.

Deductive Method

In contrast to the inductive method, the deductive method begins with known facts, or truths, and then proceeds in the opposite direction. By reasoning from a known truth(s), or general principle(s), the preacher uses existing information to reach a logical or scriptural conclusion. Textual, topical, or word studies are the common result whenever the deductive approach to sermon preparation is used.

I have noticed that most preachers have a mental tendency and a fondness towards the deductive method. Many, if not most, prefer to read the Bible and prepare their sermons with their own convictions already in mind. All they ever need to prepare a message is a scriptural text that appears to support their own personal convictions. Unfortunately, their convictions are usually nothing more than religious ideas flying around in their minds looking for a place to land. So they are forced to find a verse to light on just to prove that they have a biblical basis for what they are preaching. Preachers who prefer this approach to building sermons are typically the same ones who *use* the Bible as a tool to make their living instead of utilizing it to win souls and edify the saints. They know nothing about holding forth the word as an incorruptible seed to bring forth life.

Many preachers choose to preach topical sermons because they do not require any real effort to dig down into the text for all the hidden insights – the golden nuggets of truth that are there for the picking. It is much easier to do a broad overview of some topic and come up with a basic outline that restates a generally known biblical truth. Although the sermon may not even contradict the Bible, it doesn't effectively fulfill the true purpose of preaching. That's because it fails to **"reprove, rebuke, and exhort with all longsuffering and doctrine"** (II

Timothy 4:2). This is what I call quick and easy, in other words, lazy preaching.

As the old saying goes, "good preaching doesn't always make good doctrine." And good preaching without good doctrine is not biblical at all. In order for preaching to be right, it must be filled with sound doctrine. If not, every heretic's sermon delivered with a good speaking voice and entertaining stage antics must be considered good preaching. Not so! Great delivery should never be mistaken for great preaching. Great delivery without effective content is often full of the sound of fury, however, that often indicates that there is nothing more to the sermon than hot air and emotional jag.[2] Such characteristics are the most common components of preaching derived from the deductive approach.

I believe that there is a reason why so many Bible believing Baptist preachers have journeyed down the road of deductive preparation. Back in the early and mid-1900s, the Southern Baptist schools became known for teaching a method of inductive preaching known as expository preaching. Many Independent Baptists concluded that since the Southern Baptists were wrong about so many other things, then it stood to reason that their methods of sermon preparation must be wrong also. This led a great number of Independent Baptists to exclusively employ the deductive approach. Consequently, many of the brethren have been living on stale bread for years now because their pastors have only used textual, topical, and word studies as the basis for their preaching, or as we referred to previously, the *"take a verse and take a fit"* approach. Fortunately, there were preachers who continued to hold to the old verse-by-verse preaching method. There are still just a few today. This is an effective method. It is the old way that many preachers of the past preferred. Verse-by-verse interpretation and application is called the "homily" form of preaching. This is better than the three points and a poem approach.

Personally, I hold to a moderate expository approach. I prefer to make common sense applications that will reach today's common man; something that will speak to his or her daily needs.

Pre-Ministering Stress

Many pastors have what I call pre-ministering stress. We can picture in our minds the frustrated pastor who is experiencing this debilitating disease. He is sitting at his desk with his elbows propped up. His face is in his hands. There are hundreds of books piled up next to him and all around the room. He is obviously frustrated and at his wits end. The caption underneath this picture reads, "I can't think of anything to preach."

Unless you have pastored for a few years, you probably can't truly understand the difficulties associated with sermon preparation. Do you realize that the average pastor must come up with at least one hundred and fifty-six sermons a year? No wonder so many pastors are frustrated with sermon preparation, especially since so many of them possess no knowledge with regard to approaching a text and building a sermon. Yes, they may pray, thumb through pages of sermon books, and search commentaries. However, an effective textual study is not determined by a preacher's level of sincerity alone or by the time he puts into writing an outline.[3] Therefore, whenever he is overwhelmed by the responsibility and the task at hand, the frustrated preacher must stop and remember what preaching is really all about.

Preaching Defined

Preaching is simply the communication of truth from man to man. Preaching has two essentials elements – truth and personality.[4] I've found that planning for better preaching comes only with personal growth in the truth of the word of God. But it also involves our own individual personality. And, unfortunately, we are typically blind to our own personal weaknesses. In other words, we often fail to see what we are doing wrong and how we may be having a detrimental impact upon our own preaching. The real issue then becomes our personal character. Character is indeed the issue. If we are going to preach right we must live right. If not, preaching becomes merely a performance. Neither you nor I can play the part of a preacher in the performance called sermon delivery. We must live right. Preaching is not about maintaining the right image or the right reputation. Those are not the issues. Integrity is the issue! G. D. Boardman, the great nineteenth century preacher said this: "Sow an act, reap a habit, sow godly habits, reap character, sow character and reap a destiny."[5] Preaching all comes down to how we live our lives. We must exercise integrity as we pursue knowledge.

This is an essential key to understanding the course of action that our sermons will take. We must exercise integrity if we are going to develop our preaching skills. We must also exercise integrity if we are going to grow in our desire to effectively communicate God's message. Integrity stems from the desire to do right. Never underestimate the importance of desire. As preachers, we must continually stoke the fire within our hearts and **"stir up the gift of God, which is in thee..."** (II Timothy 1:6).

Also brethren, be sure to chase your passion, not your pension. Someone once asked me, "How do you keep your zeal and passion while sitting on the sidelines instead of the spot light of the platform?" My answer was that it's kind of like being married. I've been married twenty-nine years now to my wife Cheryl. Yes, there may be snow on the rooftop, but there is still fire in the fireplace. Never depend on the spotlight to keep you fired up for the Lord Jesus Christ. The heat must come from within, not from without.

The best biblical illustration to this point is found in Acts 1:15-26. Here we have the story of the apostle Matthias. Matthias served for three and one-half years in the background. He was never mentioned once in the four gospels. But then one day there was an opening for service and God chose Matthias to step in and fulfill the role. The story of Matthias illustrates the way our ministries should be. He was faithful, patient, and sat ready in the shadows until the time came that God put him in his place of service. Matthias' example makes it clear that you and I should make sermons while we are waiting for the opening. That kind of preparation will help to keep the fires going.

Don't get discouraged and give up. Don't set yourself up to fail. Preaching requires determination. That leads me to say that we, as preachers, should never confuse a single defeat with a final defeat. The great hall of fame basketball coach for UCLA, John Wooden, made the following statement in his book on coaching, "Do not let what you cannot do interfere with what you can do."[6]   Of all the human resources remember that the most precious is the desire to improve.

As I mentioned earlier, I believe that the preacher who utilizes a moderate expository approach can accomplish much when it comes to preaching. This method not only allows the Bible to speak for itself, but it also applies common sense. Recall Dr. Lackey's words, "God ain't in nothing that doesn't make common sense."

To start out right in our approach of expository preaching, there are three important elements that must be incorporated.

1) Observation: This requires the preacher to examine the text for every detail.
2) Interpretation: This requires the preacher to come to an understanding of the text.
3) Proclamation: This is how the preacher will express the text in the form of communication.

Observation

There is an old saying that goes like this: "Right judgment draws us a profit from all things we see."[7] This aptly applies to the benefit we will receive from rightly observing the passage used as our context. In this regard, there are two general forms of observation we must pursue.

The first form is known as the panoramic view. The panoramic view means that we must look at the larger picture. In other words, look at the text as a whole. The second form is known as the microscopic view. This view looks for details in the text itself. This is done to find out what the text is teaching and who it is about (the subject).

Bible handbooks are usually good sources to gather information on the text itself. It is also beneficial to read the chapters before and after the text you are dealing with. The object here is not to collect trivial details that bore the listeners, but details that will catch their attention.

You must remember that the Bible text never changes. It is always the same. How is it then that one preacher can see things that others can't? The difference in interpretation has to do with what they see. One preacher looks and sees nothing while the other looks and sees only what is apparent to the alert, attentive, and learned eye. Remember this does not have to do strictly with Bible knowledge. It has everything to do with a trained preaching eye. If God Almighty has given you the gift of oratory, but you don't make the effort to develop yourself by looking, practicing, training, praying, and studying in order to develop a preacher's eye and see things that others don't see, then you will never make it as a Bible preacher. Oratory and a trained eye are the Siamese twins that are effective only when they are bound together in delivering a message. If they are cut apart, one usually dies. In most cases, it is the trained eye. It is harder to see things that others don't. In fact, it is much harder than just opening your mouth and filling it with your own foot. That's why you must train yourself to see things that other preachers typically pass over every week during their approach to preparation for the pulpit.

Dr. Herbert E. Noe taught me this lost art of seeing things in the passages of the Bible that others don't see. Dr. Noe was one of the greatest expository preachers I've ever heard. I had the blessing of sitting under his ministry for three years. I heard him bring out the truths of the scriptures weekly. Dr. Noe greatly influenced my style of preaching and sermon preparation. I am eternally thankful for all that I learned from him. Notably, Dr. Bob Jones Sr. taught Dr. Noe.

The appreciation I have for all that Dr. Noe taught me became very real to me during a revival in Florida back in 1994. I was preaching out of Isaiah 28:27-28. The sermon was entitled "The Fitches, the Cummin, and the Corn." The message described different ways that God will use to break, or crush, people that He plans to use. After preaching the sermon, a few preachers told me that they appreciated it and wondered how that message came out of that particular passage of scripture. I don't say that to sound boastful. I say it because I'm just like any other preacher. I had to be taught and then I had to put what I learned into practice.

In preparing that message, I had simply done what Dr. Noe taught me to do. I used both a panoramic and a microscopic view of the scriptures. Oftentimes, this requires looking past the obvious to find a hidden meaning or truth that may not be very apparent when you first read over a particular passage. Bro. Roloff used to say this, "Two men sat behind bars, one saw mud, and the other saw stars." Do you know what the difference was between those two men? The difference was in the direction they were looking for help. One man was looking up while the other man was looking down. It was all in their observation. Always remember that observation demands the following:

- an eye for details
- a healthy learner's curiosity
- discernment as to what is worthy of close attention
- a willingness to postpone judgment
- a ruthless realism about the facts stated in the text

Personally, I do not like games. I don't mean sports, but board games. The one that I hate the most is Trivial Pursuit. There is no excitement in that game for me. It's all about who can sound off the most facts and figures. Throughout my years as a preacher, I've sat and listened to this game many times being played in the pulpit. I've listened to preachers deliver their own unique versions of trivial pursuit as they preached and recited facts and figures, but never expounded on the deep truths of the passage they were referencing. As a preacher, be careful not to confuse scriptural observations for trivial pursuits in your preaching.

Interpretation

When dealing with the textual interpretation there are basically three questions that must be answered:

1) What do we have here?
2) What does it mean?
3) What significance does it have for us?

Whenever we come to the sacred text we do not come alone. We come with God. We are His messengers and His voice. We become representatives of God to his people. We must then open the Bible with an ear to hear, a heart to accept, and the courage to deliver the message given to us from God. Before the congregation, we need to bring the Lord into the people's needs, their hopes, their problems, and their weaknesses. The preacher does not come for himself, but for them, the congregation.

How can you get focused in that direction? Just walk into the church on the Saturday before the Sunday you plan to preach. If possible, sit down in the place where the widow woman is usually seated. Sit in the seat of the one who just lost a baby, or the one who was recently divorced, or the person suffering from an illness. Look up to the pulpit from the place where the parents with the prodigal child will be sitting, or from the pew where the family sits that just buried their loved one. Sit there and consider how the message will be interpreted by them – the message that God has given you for the Lord's day.

Ask yourself this question, "What do I have here?" Examine the message. Analysis it as though you are a medical researcher hoping to find the cure for a terminal illness. Look at every detail. Be prepared to give the remedy for the malady so that when people hear you speak it doesn't sound like a message in a vacuum. Don't make it some academic or scholarly prescription that no one can interpret. The biblical text holds what they need. Be the interpreter. Interpret the word of God so that the Great Physician can speak to their hearts and pour out the balm of Gilead upon their souls. A text needs a proper interpretation so that it can minister to those who so desperately need to hear it.

When interpreting the passage, search for the writer's thoughts in the text so that the word of God can be given as manna was to those who hungered in the wilderness. Always study and pray to understand what the passage means and what it is saying.

We know that the Bible is written to every generation upon this earth. And we do realize that it is all written <u>for</u> us, but all of it is not written <u>to</u> us. Biblical preaching learns to apply each message to the needs of today, not what is going to happen in the future (unless we are dealing with prophecy). Give the people something for their hearts and their lives. Let the word of God speak to the troubles that afflict them on a daily basis. We must give out the truth of the Bible. The congregation needs to hear about the principles of justice, grace, love, obedience, and faith. Here is the message from God. Here is Heaven's viewpoint.

If we are to successfully interpret, we must be ever learning ourselves as preachers. Therefore, we need to practice drawing pictures with your words. Allow the text of the Bible to rightly interpret the Bible. Then we can focus on the significance that it holds for us today.

Our messages should focus the text so that the light shines into the lives of each individual, not just the group as a whole. Give them the meaning and interpretation of the passage as though it was personally written to them as we know that it was. Speak to individuals as though they are the only ones there, even as you address the entire congregation. This is indeed an art. Only the trained craftsmen can perform this well. A greenhorn will only address the problems of the local church. He doesn't speak to individuals from the pulpit. That is not preaching. It is only shielded cowardice. If we are to rightly interpret the text, we, as preachers, must think of our congregations, see their faces, and look into their minds. We must place ourselves in the pew to see and hear as they do. Then ask ourselves, "What can this message do for the young family just starting out, the elderly couple failing in health, the confused youth needing direction, the struggling saint needing hope, or the backslider and lost soul that need to be brought back to the cross. How will these people interpret this message that I am preparing?"

When considering how the message will be interpreted, ask yourself what benefit can come of the message you propose to preach. Why does anyone even need to hear this message? What difference can it make? As we consider these questions and meditate on the passage, we will experience at least three things. 1) We will come to a deeper understanding of the truth of the text. 2) We will come to a more sympathetic understanding of the listener and develop a more compassionate attitude. 3) We will develop a more interesting and compelling presentation of the message God has given us.

An effective preacher needs to understand the real world life of the saints that God has given us to preach to. By properly interpreting the text of the scriptures, we provide the antidote from the word of God to sooth the sufferings that stem from the human experience. With the biblical text in one hand and the needs of the congregation in the other, the preacher can begin the process of interpretation.

It is my personal conviction that no sermon is ready for preaching, not even ready to be written out, until we can express it's theme in a timely, biblical, clear as crystal interpretation. I do not think that the sermon ought to be preached until the preacher has labored and found the interpretation to be as clear as the moonlit sky of a winter night.

Proclamation

In the last chapter we briefly discussed homiletics, or speech communication. Here, I want to call your attention to the word *"hermeneutics."* This word comes from the word "Hermes," who was a messenger for the Greek gods in Greek mythology. Hermes was a messenger of eloquence. And his speech could capture the attention of the Greek gods. So when we refer to hermeneutics, we are speaking of a form of biblical interpretation that can capture the attention. To do this, a preacher must learn how to ask the right questions. Asking the right questions is vitally important. In turn, asking the wrong questions can only bring wrong answers. Therefore, one of the most critical issues involving hermeneutics is learning how to ask the right questions. Here are a few key words to consider whenever you are looking over a text: Who, What, Where, When, and Why? Consider the warning found in Jeremiah chapter 42. Use this passage to ask yourself the following:

- What is going on here?
- When is it going on?
- Where is it going on?
- Who is it going on with?
- Why is it going on here?
- What is the spiritual warning being taught?

9

Principals of Organization

We will now turn our attention to the principles of organizing a sermon outline from a passage of scripture. At this point, we must remember that when we are dealing with expository sermons, we are dealing with pure Bible passage outlines and we are preaching from them. Compared to other methods you have either heard or preached, you will find the method of expository preaching to be as different as salt is to pepper.

I have recently come to the conclusion that textual, topical, metaphorical, word studies, and any other kind of sermon preaching just doesn't get the job done. Only a moderate exposition of the scriptures will get the job done. In this chapter, the preacher and his delivery are not the main focus. Instead, it is the word of God and the scriptural text from which we will preach. Remember, the message is always greater than the messenger.

At this point, we have to move from what God said in the scriptures in order to formulate an outline and create a biblical message. Therefore, the first principle of organization is our own learning. We must make sure that we know and understand what God has said in the text. Then, we can begin the process of presentation and follow the avenue of communication.

As Olford says, "The hermeneutical hat is replaced by the homiletic hat, and the preacher now thinks about what needs to be preached."[1] When it comes to preaching a message from the Bible, organization is mandatory. The theme, thoughts, and the thrust have to be governed by the text that we are dealing with. The preacher is the one who proclaims the text's message. He is to proclaim the same thing that the text is proclaiming. To do this correctly, the preacher must once again ask the question: What are the truths of this text that need to be proclaimed?

Olford (based on W. Graham Scroggie's ideas) suggests answering these questions from the passage at hand:

1.   What is the dominating theme?
2.   What are the integrating thoughts?
3.   What is the motivating thrust?[2]

The Dominating Theme

G. Campbell Morgan said that there are three essential components in preaching, "truth, clarity, and passion"[3] with truth being preeminent. He was referring to the truth of the text. It is the central idea and serves as the unifying element of the sermon. We recognize it as the subject matter of the message. Truth must always master our messages. The only way to do this is to make sure that we keep the dominating theme as our guide throughout the whole preparation of the message. When the text has been studied and the truth has been recognized, then "the dominating theme should come right out of the text,"[4] right off the pages of God's word.

The Integrating Thoughts

Olford commenting:

> The integrating thoughts should likewise come right out
> of the text, expressing what the text says about the
> dominating theme. A list of such thoughts, as we will
> see, helps to provide structure, movement, and
> interrelatedness to the message. A message must move;
> you can't say everything at the same time! There has to
> be sequence, and the guiding principle of the sequence
> and movement of a message should be the truth-
> movement of the text.[5]

There has to be sequence in the sermon. It needs stepping-
stones in order to build a bridge from the Bible to the pew.
The integrating thoughts serve as points or "the thinking of the
text."[6]

The Motivating Thrust

Olford again:

> The motivating thrust has to do with the challenge, the
> call, the appeal, the appropriate cumulative application of
> the text. G. Campbell Morgan refers to the need for
> passion in preaching. The two words *motivating* and
> *thrust* are passionate words. They are also purposeful
> words. The motivating thrust or the 'call' of the text,
> guides the preacher in clarifying the *purpose* of the
> message. What is this message *to do?* It is good to
> clarify this motivating thrust, to indicate where the
> message is going from first to last. This indicates the
> purpose and the passion of the message, and hopefully of
> the preacher as well. . . . Truth must dominate and
> permeate the message. There must be an unfolding, and
> explanation of the truth in some form of sequence. [7]

I know that there are many who believe that outlines are
not of God. Where I live and in the places I minister that is the
general thought. Nonetheless, outlines are valuable because
they help to bring clarity to the message. Clarity is the goal in
this regard. A clear presentation of integrated thoughts is
essential. The motivating thrust, although possibly emphasized

in the conclusion, should always be directed in line with the purpose and passion of the message.

Finding the Dominating Theme

To find the dominating theme, or the central idea, you must look for phrases, repetitions, ideas, and other recurring points. Sometimes the theme or central idea does not stand out. In those cases, the preacher must gain a sense of the theme from the context of the passage. It is a good practice to write down the dominating theme. The more precise the better it is. Write down the thoughts, the points, or the textual movements in sequence.

The outline must always stay faithful to the text. The thoughts must also come from the text. They should not be imposed or forced to fit into the text. A good outline should reflect only the thoughts of the text.

It may be good to put the verses, sentences, phrases, or words, and the specific textual basis for the point, right beside each point as you write them down. Your outline should have a flow to it as a result of your textual investigation. No matter how beautiful the outline or logical the outline is, it is not good if it does not express the thoughts of the text. It has been said many times, "I have a good outline, and if God gets in it, it will be a good message." How true!

To get God into an outline, the primary emphasis has to be biblical and come directly from the text itself. But it must also be logical. We are not preaching about some sophisticated form of philosophical conjecture. We are preaching about understandable logic. The message must be something that the common man can sink his teeth into. As we have already discussed – it is basic common sense logic. This logic has to be captured from the text and put into the outline.

Olford (*Anointed Expository Preaching* pages 146-151) gives an example of sermon building based on Matthew 28:16-20. Referring back to the three-fold process, the first question to be answered is: "What is the dominating theme?"

In this respective passage, we know that the theme is the Lord's Great Commission. So we write it down.

Theme: Our Lord's great commission or our Lord's great commission given to His disciples.

Next, we establish the integrating thoughts:

- Eleven disciples.
- An appointed mountain.
- Are you worshipping or doubting today?
- Jesus has all authority.
- We should make disciples Jesus' way.
- Jesus is always with us.
- Make disciples.
- To make good disciples you must be a good disciple.

Now this format could be used for preaching but there is a problem. The relationship between each point is not clear and does not follow a distinct pattern. There is no smooth flow or transition between the key ideas. An outline like this will only be good as a springboard. It will bounce you around from one point to another. More work is required to prepare this outline the right way. Consider the following outline compared to the one above.

I. Our Lord's Authority for the Great Commission – Mt. 28:18
II. Our Lord's Strategy for the Great Commission – Mt. 28:19-20a
III. Our Lord's Availability for the Great Commission – Mt. 28:20b

-OR-

I. The Power of the Lord for His Great Commission – Mt. 28: 18

II. The Program of the Lord for His Great
Commission – Mt. 28:19-20a

III. The Presence of the Lord for His Great
Commission – Mt. 28:20b

By weaving the theme of the Great Commission throughout the outline, you enable the listeners to follow you as you guide them through the passage. This gives the Bible a clear voice. Each point becomes clear. It is important for preachers to keep the message clear and plain.

Most (if not all) sermons need to be tailored in order to keep things flowing with a logical theme. The thing that you should strive for is simplicity. You should never want to *sacrifice* truth, but we do want to *simplify* truth. You should, therefore, limit the number of primary points and levels of sermon structure as much as possible. Once again, common sense and experience will guide you and help you to see when the main points and sub-points are becoming too many and too long.

The outline must be heard. This is done with the use of symmetrical construction, rhythm, and alliteration. All of these are great for helping people to hear the outline. Investing a little work to fashion the outline is a mandatory prerequisite for communicating the message effectively.

People should not only hear the outline, they must see it as well. This is important. People will see the message with words, and they will also see it by watching you. Your facial expressions, your tone, your excitement (or lack of excitement) will be seen as well as heard. You, the preacher, must not only pronounce the message, you must portray it so that others will see it come to life. You don't do this by the use of overhead projectors. You do this with words. You will have to create word pictures. Remember that skeletal outlines have no meat on them.

We must make the transition from revealed truth in the passage to what needs to be said to proclaim that truth. This step requires the preacher to frame the message. Put it in context and make it real in the eyes and ears of the congregation. Use your outline as a tool to accomplish the task. Make it interesting and make it logical. As it comes to life it will be a channel through which the word of God can change lives. However, it must always be in subjection to the Bible text. It is the Bible that works to change lives, not our outlines. Keep your emphasis in the right place.

It is not an easy task to be a preacher. It is more than just being a man who proclaims truth. God manifests His Word through PREACHING. Preaching is what we shall do and what we must do until He comes back or we go up.

John Newton said:

> My main theme in preaching is to break the hard heart and to heal the broken one. I love a serious preacher; one who speaks for my sake and not his own. One who seeks my salvation; not his own vain glory. I love a preacher who knows how to clothe his thoughts with his words and by doing so promotes virtue and truth. Nothing to me is more detestable than a professed declaimer who retails his discourse as a quack does his medicine.

The best sermon you'll ever preach will not be the one where everyone approaches you afterwards to tell you how great you are. Neither will it be a one that leaves you believing all the great things that folks may be saying about you. The best sermon will be the one that has folks departing from the meetinghouse thoughtful and serious, and hastening to be alone.

The following poem reveals what successful preaching is really about:

> If you can preach when scowling faces meet your gaze,
> If you can smile when frowns are evident upon apace,
> If you can scatter cheer, and sullen gloom supplant,
> If you can give the pessimist a different slant,
> If you can still press on when every move is blocked,
> If you can tilt your chin when so-and-so has balked,
> If you can take dictation from the powers that be,

If you can rise above the petty things you see,
If you can plan for bigger things and stand alone,
If you can rest your weary head upon a stone,
If you can grip the hand which dealt the cruel blow,
If you can walk the second mile and love bestow,
If you can weep with saddened souls who truly weep,
If you can laugh with those whose festive hours keep,
If you can stick, let come what may, to God's own Book,
If you can to its sacred pages ever look,
If you can say "Thus saith the Lord", and know it's true,
If you can love the Gentile and the Jew,
If you can preach on Sunday with an empty purse,
If you can make your shabby suit look none the worse,
If you can drive your ancient car with self-respect,
If you can let them pass, and keep your head erect,
If you can thrill at being loved for Jesus sake,
If you can play the hectic game of give and take,
If you can lead the sinner to the cleansing flood,
If you can preach redemption through His precious blood,
If you can build for time and eternity,
If you can say at last, Thine shall the glory be
If you can do all this, O Mortal Creature,
You are in fact, as well as name, a WORTHY PREACHER. Anonymous [8]

10

Finalizing the Message

We know that a God called preacher doesn't preach to impress people with his oratory skills. Nonetheless, it is still important for a preacher to learn "to choose the best way to communicate the truth for which and to which he is responsible."[1] Words used appropriately can empower your effectiveness. Words are the building blocks of explanations, applications, and illustrations that are capable of capturing the attention of your listeners.

Keep in mind that the presentation of the message (on your part) is subject to change depending on location and the background of your listeners, but the message from the word of God should never be changed or tampered with.

With the theme, thoughts, and thrust of the message as your guide, you can begin to pray, think, and write the sermon. A message can develop and be formed in many ways, but the priority is to proclaim the truth of the text. For the purpose of discussion, as well as to provide a pattern, this section is divided into three separate components in order to map out the sermon preparation process: 1) introduction 2) exposition, and 3) conclusion.

The Introduction

Olford explaining the purpose of the introduction:

> The introduction is more than just the first words or sentences of a sermon. It is the wording that presents the message and the messenger to the particular audience being addressed. The introduction serves, also, as a verbal transition from whatever has taken place in the experience of the listeners to the event of preaching. So, besides introducing the dominating theme of the message appropriately, the introduction actually begins a new activity to which people will and must respond. Because of the unique nature of every preaching occasion, the introduction to the same basic message may differ substantially on different occasions.[2]

As you begin the message, be conscious of the time factor. Keep the time in mind. Dr. Noe taught me a real simple rule of thumb to follow whenever it comes time to stand in the pulpit. Pray Up – Study Up – Stand Up – Speak Up – and then Shut Up. Now in all my years of preaching, I've heard many good preachers say more in twenty to thirty minutes than most of those who require an hour and a half. This reminds me of the times back in the 1970s and early 1980s when Dr. Lackey's church held the old-fashioned camp meetings in White Plains, NC. During those meetings, he would always give the speakers a time limit.

I was a young preacher back then and I can still hear those preachers protesting because they only had twenty minutes to give their sermon. Some would say. "I can't preach this message in twenty minutes." Dr. Lackey would reply, "You could if you were on that radio." I learned a great lesson from him about time and climate. In fact, I learned a lot by simply watching and listening to him preach over the last few years of his life. He taught me the things that you can't teach to young preachers, especially the ones that think they already have all the answers. With that said, train yourself not to be a Pharaoh-styled preacher. Let the people go. And if you are called on to preach, keep your eye on the clock and be respectful of other people's time. Be a good and attentive messenger.

There are two more things you need even with a good introduction: "the background of the text, and the burden of the message."[3]

The background information is used to reveal the very nature of the text as given by God and it also helps the hearers to get a better knowledge of the text. It sets the stage for the sermon you are about to deliver and it points in the direction you are asking the listeners to look.

However, if you are not cautious, the introduction can waste time, weigh down your listeners with too much historical information, and ultimately cause their minds to start drifting off before you ever get to your first point.

The introduction should also present the listeners with the subject (the dominating theme) and call their attention to the burden, which will serve as the thrust of the message. The intent here is to let the congregation know not only what you are preaching, but why you are preaching it as well. It is important to give a clear, honest, and bold proclamation of what you will expound upon and what the goal of the message is. However, don't attempt to provide all the answers to the questions raised by the introduction. Those will be answered from the word of God as the sermon progresses. As a preacher, you will need to point out that the answer can be found in God's word. The answer is not found in the preacher. The answer is found in the Bible.

Once you have communicated the <u>why</u> of your sermon, you should then be sure to emphasize the seriousness and critical nature of the message you want to express. You yourself, as the preacher, must sense the critical and vital aspect of the message you intend to preach. Only then can you declare it as a message of utmost importance. In order for the hearers to embrace it, they must sense your passion and seriousness from the onset of the message. This passion must start within the introduction.[4]

We are not standing up to preach for people because we are driven by the need for popularity or prestige; nor are we preaching for money. When money becomes your banner for preaching, then you can't afford to preach. We preach so that the truth might be received and that God can be pleased as people respond in obedience.

Within the introduction, promptly communicate your fervor. Say what needs to be said and then move on to the body of the message. There must be a continuous movement of the message. Focus on communicating the background of the text, presenting the dominating theme, and then establish the burden of the message.

Every preacher has a different style when it comes to this. Personally, I prefer to read the text first and then call on someone from the audience to pray over the text. I believe this approach accomplishes two things 1) it brings the pulpit and the pew together before the text, and 2) it gives the preacher one last chance to look over his introduction before starting the message.

As you prepare, remember the importance of the introduction. The opening and closing of the message are vitally important to the effectiveness of the message. Don't worry. When you use an expository style of preaching, the text will take care of itself in the body of the message. The scripture will take care of itself. You must concentrate on taking care of the opening and the closing of the message.

Many preachers seem to get stuck as they think about the introduction of messages. If that applies to you, then move on to the first point, which you already have waiting for you in the text that you've been studying. If you're one that has a tendency to rush forward to the conclusion rather than thinking it through, then consider starting with the conclusion. You will have to discover what works best for you individually. We will now move the sermon from the introduction to the exposition of the message.

The Exposition

The purpose of the exposition is to expound on the truths contained within the biblical text using explanatory methods. The Bible itself becomes the basis of textual authority. Your outline will serve as the guide leading you down the trail toward the substance of the message. As long as the outline comes directly out of the text and represents the flow and pattern of the passage, it will lead and direct you in your efforts to reveal, declare, explain, and demonstrate the truth of the text itself.

As you proceed from the introduction into the body of the message, a series of statements will be required to accommodate the transition. If you, as the preacher, are struggling for the right transitional wording, you must realize that you already have at your disposal the authority of the whole universe, the 1611 Authorized Version. Don't forget that. When you go to stand in the pulpit, you cannot afford to be bashful or feel intimidated.

Now, as I mentioned, the opening and closing are critical in the development of the message. They are, in fact, a preacher's main tools. Albeit, you must still make sure that you handle the exposition of the text properly so that the scripture is allowed to take care of itself. Haddon W. Robinson gives a number of very helpful points with regard to constructing the expository message. An expository message must give 1) an idea to be explained, 2) a proposition to be proved, 3) a principle to be applied, 4) a subject to be completed, and 5) a story to be told.[5] Those are five good points to keep in mind as you prepare your messages. They will help you to establish solid boundaries around the text of your messages and also deter you from running rabbits and getting sidetracked off of your main points.

The truth must be allowed to master the sermon while the biblical text masters the truth. You, the preacher, must find ways to express the truth. By doing this, you allow the Bible to support and back up what you're saying. The Bible says,

"Let all things be done decently and in order" (1 Corinthians 14:40). You should apply that verse to your sermon outline. If there is anything that needs to be done decently and in order it is a Bible message. Gibbs described it best when he wrote:

> Many a sermon has been lost on an audience because of a lack of order in it. Many good things were said, but these were so jumbled up that only a discerning mind could discover them. Scrambled addresses, like scrambled eggs, soon become a very monotonous diet.[6]

The fact of the matter is that we cannot divorce the preacher from his preaching. In essence, the man is his message, the preacher is his proclamation, and the speaker is his sermon. It is the man behind the message that determines its weight. For in this endeavor, as in everything else, quality not quantity is preferred. The Stony Brook School has an excellent motto: "Character before career." Gibbs quoting Ray:

> There may have been a great expositor who was not a great preacher, but there has never been a great preacher who was not a great expositor.[7]

In recent years, those two truths have helped me come to realize just how much my preaching may have helped grow attendance in the surrounding churches of Catawba Valley North Carolina. You see, it wasn't that people couldn't take the truth of the word of God. No, it was the fact that they couldn't take my adolescence when it came to preaching. Fortunately, there were a few old preachers around who tolerated me. There were a few older and well-seasoned preachers who were willing to put up with me in spite of my braggadocios braying. They let me learn from them. They were patient enough to teach me and give me pointers from their personal experiences. Instead of shunning me and letting me go off on my own way, they helped me as they taught by

example just how to deliver an effective message. I am
eternally thankful to men such as Dr. Jack Woods, Bro. Maze
Jackson, Dr. Harold Sightler, Dr. Percy Ray, Dr. Paul
Vanaman, and Dr. Bob Jones Sr.

I still remember staying up late at night listening to
WMUU on the radio as Dr. Bob Jones, Sr. delivered his
chapel talks. I can recall many other good preachers that I
listened to in years gone by. I could give their names and you
probably wouldn't recognize who they are. But God knows
them and I sincerely believe that God sent them in my
direction just as He sent Samuel to Eli. These are the men that
I learned from over the years as God was making me into a
preacher.

Those are the old-path preachers that I mentioned earlier.
They preached in the old-fashioned expository style. They
would have had nothing to do with this lazy, "advanced" form
of Bible presentation that many people call preaching today.
The expository method is better because it gives a preacher an
advantage in his sermon delivery. However, a preacher must
learn to recognize what those advantages are. Again, we can
refer back to Gibbs, who listed several key benefits from the
expository style:

- It puts the supreme emphasis on the word
  of God itself.
- It makes for a broad knowledge of the
  scriptures as a whole.
- It provides an opportunity for speaking on
  many passages which would otherwise be
  neglected.
- It will also make for variety in the ministry
  of the Word.
- It enables the preacher to deal with current
  evils.
- It will deliver the preacher from the
  tendency to a fanciful use, or abuse of
  isolated texts.

- It will furnish the preacher with enough material for a lifetime of preaching.[8]

I would like to add one more point to Gibbs' list:

- It will teach the Bible at the same time that it is being preached.

Next we will look at the three ways to accomplish the exposition: 1) the explanation, 2) the illustration, and 3) the application.

The exposition contains the *explanation* of the message. At this point in the sermon, it is necessary to present the essence of the textual truth that is being spoken and to provide a clear explanation. As a preacher, you should limit yourself to address only the text that you are speaking on, regardless of whether it is a clause, a phrase, a passage, a verse, or several verses. This is the point where you begin to draw the word picture for the congregation from the passage. The goal is to explain. Keep that goal in mind.

You should already be familiar with the passage because you have been personally dealing with the subject text for a few hours or so through prayer and study. But, your listeners have not. They have only heard you read the passage. They will not be as aware of the treasures that you have already discovered in the particular scripture. It doesn't matter if you are preaching on prophesy, Christian living, soul-winning or directly to the lost, you must make it your second nature to lift up the biblical periscope so that all can see what you are about to preach. I call this part "unpacking the treasure chest of truth." It is something that you must do for your congregation.

This is where you have to apply the good old-fashioned common sense that I told you about. If not, you can easily lose the congregation by putting them to a state of melancholy with your much speaking. If you don't develop an ability to open the message well, then the rest of the sermon will be just like so many that we've all heard before. Here a little and there a little, but lacking substance, except for the ignorant thoughts that confuse and aggravate the listeners with repetitious rhetoric that can't help or enlighten them.

One way to develop this part of your message is to "learn from great preachers and teachers by examining how they actually explain the truths, concepts, and points they are making."[9]

Now in order to step into this part of the message, I like to use one-liners. For example, I'll make a statement like this: "Let's make down home country sense out of this," or "Wait a minute," and then I'll bring a question to the audience. This is a technique I learned from Dr. Bob Jones Sr. He perfected this skill in his own sermons. It allowed the hearers to see where the message was going and provided a platform for them to get on board. If I am in a country church, I might say, "Let's look at this passage and see what learning we can get from it." I'll usually identify that statement as my backwoods English. That kind of a statement adds a little humor and helps to set people at ease. I've found that people will listen better if they are set at ease or, if nothing else, perceive that they are smarter than the preacher. It is human nature to compare ones self with others in order to relate or to lift up yourself to the one doing the speaking. So we must learn not only to isolate the elements of the passage and capture the attention of the audience, but also draw their attention so that all can see how they relate to the flow of the text.

Illustrations are important components of the exposition. The illustration can be viewed as the twin brother to explanation. In Nehemiah 8:8, the preachers **"gave the sense"** to what was being read from the scriptures. **"Gave the sense"** is a Bible phrase. That is exactly what the illustration should accomplish. It should help the explanation make sense.

Now there are only a few real masters when it comes to this delicate part of the sermon. One of the best was the late Dr. Jack Woods. Dr. Woods was a master at personal illustrations. He used illustrations to get people to laugh and feel at ease. After the people let their guard down he could get through to their hearts. The humorous illustrations captured the congregation's interest and set them up for the delivery of the main point of the message. Illustrations are priceless tools, especially in the hands of experts.

One thing that can make your illustrations more valuable is timing; knowing right when to use them. They can bring the scriptures to life in the minds of the congregation. However, learning the exact moment to throw in the most pertinent illustration requires almost a sixth sense. This is something you must learn to develop. You'll need to be able to determine when more explanation is needed to help the text come to life.

The sources for illustration materials are numerous. My first source for illustrations comes from my own personal experiences. I believe a preacher's personal experience can provide the best kind of illustration. But let me stop here and say this. You cannot preach above your own experiences. Some may say, "Preacher, you have never experienced heaven, hell, etc. So how can you preach on those things?" Well, the first thing all of us must experience is common sense. When I say that you cannot preach above your experience, I mean you must be able to speak from your own experiences in life. If you can't, then it will be extremely difficult for you to impart the truth of a particular point or passage to others.

If you have an ear for preaching (and many people today don't) all you have to do is listen. Listen to preachers and you'll usually hear the same illustrations coming from different preachers all over this country and the world. Don't be that kind of preacher. Don't keep using the same illustrations over and over again in different sermons. Search and find new ones. That's part of staying fresh.

Now if you need other illustrations, you can always look to the Bible. The Bible is a great source. "By using biblical material you expose or remind people of other biblical texts and help them see how Scripture can interpret Scripture."[10]

There are plenty of books available that are filled with illustrations, short stories, quotes, etc. You can also get illustrations from the daily newspaper and current events. Read historical accounts, literature, hymns, poetry, and books by other preachers. Take advantage of resource books and computer programs. The list is long. Just make sure that the illustrations you use are from credible sources.

The explanation part of the sermon paints the picture of the text. The illustrations must be used to personalize it. That's why they are so important. Nonetheless, it should only be used to point out what is already obvious from the explanation. And if the point of the illustration is not obvious, then it is not useful and becomes needless rhetoric. The following pointers will help you in your use of illustrations:

Become well rehearsed in communicating the illustrations that you want to use. If you have to illustrate the illustration, then you have selected the wrong one for sure. And whatever you do, please don't over-illustrate, lest you divert everyone's attention from the text.

Only select words that picture the truth. Instead of over-cooking illustrations, you as a preacher can improve your messages by using a good choice of words to make the truth easier to see and recognize. This can be just as helpful to the listeners as a good illustration. Remember, the human soul cannot take a steady diet of illustrations. Only the word of God can change and enlighten the hearts of men. Therefore, learn to have a balance in your preaching with illustrations. Always use illustrations, but never let them outweigh the text. Again, illustrations should only be used to bring the text to life in the hearts of those who are listening.

Let your illustration capture the listener's attention. A masterpiece illustration draws a picture that people can clearly see and it doesn't shut down a person's thoughts. You will be able to tell. Whenever you look in their eyes and see that faraway look, you'll know that they are no longer listening. The human mind shuts down when it is overloaded with illustrations.

Implement the five parts of an effective verbal illustration. Wayne McDill quotes Eugene Lowry on his comment about how to tell a story. He writes:

> In whatever type of narrative plot, the event of the story moves from a bind, a felt discrepancy, an itch born of ambiguity, and moves towards the solution, a release from the ambiguous mystery, the scratch that makes it right.[11]

Look at your illustrations and make sure that they contain these five elements to emphasize the point you want to get across, 1) the situation of the problem, 2) the stress of the problem, 3) the search of the problem, 4) the solution of the problem, and 5) the new situation of the problem. Using this pattern in telling an illustration will assist you in building a mental sketch. When rightly applied, the preacher will present the problem and its resolution to the listener. It can then be applied in context of the biblical truth being expounded upon.

The well-tuned preacher must know his message, his audience, and his own preaching strengths and weaknesses. Once an illustration has made its impact in the sermon, leave it there. Don't go back to it again just to get another "A-men."

An effective sermon will also contain the *application*. When you apply a message, you simply communicate to the listeners what the Bible text is speaking on to them. Application brings the text to a personal level. You relate the Bible to the lives of the people living today. This doesn't mean that you should back your listeners into a corner without giving them a way out. Should you give them biblical truths? Yes. Should you illustrate your text? Yes. But, more importantly, take the appropriate steps that will get them to God. Help them to apply the truth so that they can be led to respond to the message.

I encourage you to apply the message throughout the sermon. Make the truths of the message personally relevant to each person listening. The congregation should sense the importance of the application throughout each part as the message proceeds. But, if the application is not your strength, then you should write it out and read it continuously over and over again until you have it embedded in your soul. Then you will be able to use it to bring sinners and saints to God.

Once you learn how to apply the text well, you will be able to throw out the net and bring in the catch. If you miss the application, then no matter how good your outline is and no matter how you have learned to master illustrations, you will still miss the whole purpose and intent of preaching.

Applications must be made at the right time in the message. Timing is the pearl of great price when it comes to preaching. It is the balm of Gilead. It is the alabaster box that we must learn to break so that we may pour the ointment over our Master's head and allow the fragrance to fill the whole house. As Dr. Bryan Chapell once said:

> Preachers that cannot differentiate between a scriptural mandate and a good suggestion drain biblical power from their ministries. You must make sure that the scriptures, not you, demand what your application requires.[12]

As I said before, we are preaching for eternity. Learn how to do it right so that souls are not deprived of the truth of God's word because we neglected to fine-tune our preaching gift. Be thorough as you build the message. Do not leave loose threads of thought hanging from your sermon. This means you must not only focus on effectiveness, but efficiency as well given the time you have to preach.

To master this ability, you must: a) Make sure each thought is completed in the sermon. b) Keep moving on, implementing a smooth transition from one facet of the text to the next. Don't get stuck on one good point and end up excluding other pertinent points. They should all add up to complete the message. c) Harness the sense of movement occurring in each section of the message. Learn to feel it. What you can't feel, you can't preach. d) Keep the message tied together all the way, not just at the end. Don't attempt to rope all the cattle with one thought at the end. Keep the sermon together or you will miss the whole herd. e) Remember that each and every point is critical and calls for a textual explanation, an illustration (if necessary), and an application. f) Nothing in the passage of scripture is extraneous or insignificant. g) If you sense that there is something in the outline that is not needed, even as you are preaching the message, delete it. It may be that the thought you had during the preparation will not fit well as you are actually standing there delivering the message. If so, then divorce that thought right away before it gets you off of the subject. Remember that your outline is only intended to serve as a guide. Don't be rigidly bound by it. h) Cover the text fairly, but maintain clarity throughout the exposition. In other words, don't go so deep that you drown the listeners long before the Lord opens the Red Sea to cross over. Keep it simple, scriptural, and sensible.

The Conclusion

This is one of the most important parts of the message. It "clarifies, exhorts, and invites a response appropriate to the truth that has been declared."[13]   Even if you're not a great preacher or speaker, and many of us are not, strive to be a good closer. Get good at throwing the net. Don't bring it up until you feel the fish bumping into it from the inside. The same thing applies to throwing the net for baitfish or mullet. You can lose plenty of fish if you're not careful when you go to draw the net. Part of being a good fisherman is to know how to bring in the catch.

Use exhortation. Don't switch hats at this point in the message. Keep following through from the opening to this point of conclusion. After a biblical exhortation has been presented, you the preacher, should then instruct, guide, and invite a response.

The preacher must know how to effectively conclude the message and lead it into the invitation. This is always a divine, holy, and significant event in the service. More than anything, you must learn to be sensitive to the Holy Spirit of God. Learn to sense how God is moving in the hearts of the congregation. The invitation time provides an opportunity for people to make a decision, to settle something, to take that first step of obedience, and to get back into their relationship with God.

There are many different ways to give an invitation at the end of a sermon. The manner changes from location to location. There is never a set plan. It seems that God's people are so programmed by the modern-day way of giving an invitation that when the preacher says, "Let's stand and pray," the people start grabbing the song books and looking for "Just As I Am." There is no God in it at all. So, see what works best for the area you are in, but most of all, let God get into the invitation.

Years ago, we used to hold two-week revivals. We would have one preacher preach throughout the first week and then another preacher would come in and finish up the second week. Many times, I would tell the first preacher not to give an invitation at all for the first week. This would let the people go home and think about what they had heard. That strategy has always worked well in North Carolina. Here is why.

When the second preacher came in and preached his first sermon, I would ask him to be sure and give an invitation beginning the first night. During that second week, it was not unusual to see sinners get saved and to watch saints come to the altar to get right. To say the least, the second week of revival was usually the time when we would experience a real outpouring of the Holy Spirit like the kind many people have heard about in North Carolina revivals. It happened because God was given time to work and to soften the hearts of the people. It had nothing to do with going through the motions of extending an invitation at the end of a service. That's why the invitation time should never be rushed nor should it be overplayed or stretched out just to get a response.

John R. Stott in *The Preachers Portrait* said:

It is wrong to deny our own responsibility in the application of the Word. All great preachers understand this. They focus on the conclusion, on the application of the text. This is what the Puritans called preaching through to the heart.[14]

As preachers, we must never issue an appeal, the invitation, without first making the proclamation. Then, to follow this same thought, we must never make a proclamation without then issuing an appeal, if God leads us to do so in the service.

It is not enough simply to teach the gospel. We must urge men to embrace it. It is true that some preachers are better sowers than others, while some are better reapers. But whether you are a good sower or a good reaper, every preacher behind the pulpit must preach the Word.

Being aware of this procession, let's identify four effective ways to conclude with a sermon invitation:

1) <u>The Public Invitation</u>: This invitation is given directly at the close of the message. It is the public call to both sinners and saints to come to the altar and respond to the message that they have heard.

2) <u>After-Meeting Method</u>: Persuade those who may not have come forward publicly to do so after the service. There are a million reasons why some folks will not come forward in a crowd. They may be shy or simply uncomfortable. Try to persuade those who wanted to come, but did not, to linger after the service. This may provide you with an opportunity to do personal work and deal with them after the message is presented.

3) <u>Counseling Method</u>: This involves one-on-one interaction with those seeking help in spiritual matters.

4) <u>Follow-up Method</u>: This can be done by mail, phone, or personal visitation during the week following the service. Always give out visitor cards to people visiting your service. Keep a record of their attendance so that you can visit with them later on in the week.

Remember that obedience and revelation travel in parallel lines. As lost sinners and saved Christians obey what they have heard from God's word, God reveals truth. Conversely, when people refuse to listen to God and refuse to obey, then He will withhold further light on the truth. You may be able to gather second-hand information, notes of sermon outlines or anything else you want, but when God withholds revelation there will be no progress in spiritual matters and there will not be any new births. So whether or not you see any outward response evident in the service, inward response is a critical part of the preaching service. Never forget that "Light rejected becomes lightening." Or as others have said – Light obeyed bringeth light. Light rejected bringeth night!

11

The Delivery

When examining the delivery of a sermon, we must first give consideration to the man making the delivery, the preacher himself. It is my opinion that a man must possess the God given gift to preach. The man who does not possess a natural, inherent gift for delivery should not be allowed in the pulpit. Second, a preacher must also be a man of sincerity and truth. Everything false and superfluous must be banished from the pulpit. A trumpet doesn't need to be made of silver to in order to blow. An old ram's horn will do. However, the ram's horn must be durable. That is why a preacher must also be committed to the cause of Christ and committed to the work that God has called him to do. Just like the ram's horn, he should be capable of withstanding rough usage over many years.

Trumpets are for war campaigns and for conflicts, not for fashion runways. They have a distinguishable sound, so does the sound of truth. The sound of truth isn't dependent upon the way your own unique voice sounds. As I mentioned earlier, whether your talk is considered country or whether it is considered eloquent articulation, the important thing to remember is that your voice should be natural (your own, not imitated) and it should be taken care of so that it will last you through the years.

Being natural and relaxed is important when it comes to delivering a message from the pulpit. That is why you should do what comes naturally for you. You are called to preach, not to mimic. Trying to imitate somebody else is perhaps the highest form of theological treason and it is an insult to common decency. Intimidating someone in the pulpit is nothing more than Hollywood acting. It is playing the role of an actor rather than being a voice for God crying in the wilderness. John Wesley once stated that a preacher should beware of anything that feels awkward as it pertains to his gestures, phrases, or pronunciation. He's right. When you try to imitate someone else rather than be yourself, you place yourself in a most awkward and vicarious position. And your listeners will recognize the fact that you are concerned more with giving a good performance than with being a good preacher. Learn first of all to be yourself.

The Practical Voice

Part of being yourself means that you must develop your own God-given voice. Development involves learning to use your voice in a practical manner. As a practical preacher, recognize the fact that preaching isn't about yelling and screaming at the top of your lungs. It is about using your voice as a tool, which involves proper projection, breathing, and inflection. It requires you to learn to speak from your mouth, not your throat.

One of the greatest ways to undermine your preaching is to continually speak from the throat instead of the mouth. That is not a very practical way to preach. Let me warn you now. You will destroy your vocal chords quickly if you don't learn how to preach in the right manner. In Matthew 5:2, we read that when Jesus preached, **"he opened his mouth."** Recognize the importance of opening wide the doors from which godly truths shall come forth.

Many good men and great preachers have ruined their throats prematurely simply because they never learned to speak from their diaphragm. Many in their latter years needed microphones in order to be heard. Their low guttural blasts couldn't be heard past the first six pews. That is a tragedy. I speak from experience. There have been times in the past when I myself have preached so hard in a meeting that after the first or second night my voice felt so hoarse that it seemed I couldn't go on. This is because I did not know the right way to speak when I was preaching. Over the years I have learned better.

Having a raspy voice isn't the mark of a well-schooled, advanced preacher. It is not a sign of seniority among the ranks of preachers. All a raspy preaching voice means is that the man never learned to preach from his diaphragm. One of the best ways to find out just how you preach is by street preaching. After you tear up your throat a few times yelling from a street corner, you'll learn the importance of learning to preach from your belly.

The best way to learn this while you are speaking is to push out using your stomach. Speaking from the diaphragm has a way of opening up the lungs and taking the pressure off of the throat. If you're looking for volume then that is the way to get it. You always want to speak so that you can be heard. Let your words fall upon the ears of the listener so that they have a chance to do their work. The goal is not for you to break the backs of the listeners in your vehement rage. The congregation shouldn't have to run to keep up with what you are saying. Neither should they have to bear the miserable malady of a slow, inactive monologue. There is the right balance. Use caution when you feel yourself slowing down to a one mph pace or whenever you put on the gas and accelerate up to 1,000. Here is what I mean:

The one mph pace is a slow speech, somewhat like a slow fire. You might bless the listeners by what gets said, but quite frankly, a slow preacher typically is a real drag to listen to. Conversely, the one thousand mph delivery is the other excessive end of the spectrum. It is a rapid-fire delivery that tears and raves into what is usually nothing more than a rant. That kind of preaching is quite inexcusable. It is not effective and powerful. That kind of delivery does nothing more than transform what should be an army of words into an uncontrollable mob that drowns out the senses with high decibel noise. An un-muffled automobile sounds just as bad as the high squeaking sound of an un-oiled rocking horse.

The Prepared Voice

General George S. Patton said, "Wars are won by men with strong wills to win and strong bodies."[1] That great WWII general recognized the significance of a sound mind and a sound body in battle. In the battle for the souls of men they are equally as important. Do you realize that your vocal chords are part of your body? The important question, however, is this: Is your whole body, not just your voice, prepared to preach?

You see, your vocal chords are not the only part of your body that contributes to your ability to preach. As a preacher, you will need to make sure that you not only maintain a strong will, but also a strong body that is able to bear up under the stress and demands that come with preaching. This kind of self-discipline requires you to constantly keep your body under subjection. A prepared body is the prerequisite for a prepared voice. This process of preparation begins in the mind. The mind must keep the body under subjection (1 Corinthians 9:27).

Never let the body control the mind. Mind power, word power, speaking power, and ultimately preaching power come from the brain. All of these are dependent upon appropriate breathing. Breathing is how the brain gets its power. The lungs supply oxygen. Air gets into the blood system and then feeds oxygen back to the brain. It is a well-developed automatic physiological process that God designed to work within you. It should be a natural process. So natural that your audience ought not to know that you're breathing at all when you preach. When you preach, the process of breathing should be as unobserved as the circulation of the blood in your veins.

Something is wrong whenever this natural function called breathing causes you to stop and take a hiatus in your message because your body has to labor so hard to maintain your oxygen supply. If you find that you need more lung power it isn't hard to develop. In fact, you can practically double your lungpower by taking and holding a deep breath periodically throughout the day. Hold those deep breaths as long as possible and then exhale. This is a very simple exercise that will work to give you lungpower.

Whatever you do, don't fall into the profile of today's typical preacher – overweight and out of shape. There is only one way to avoid that profile – exercise regularly throughout the week, daily if possible. The men in the pulpit who are the most prone to a heart attack all have one thing in common – a large tire around the middle. This one physical characteristic describes too many preachers today. It really is a shame. In my opinion, there is nothing worse than to hear a three hundred pound preacher stand up and preach against women wearing pants. The first thing that kind of messenger needs to do is to start studying how to put a knife to his own throat (Proverbs 23:2).

Being in shape and staying healthy is important for a preacher. His tools called the voice and the throat rely on oxygen. You may have noticed that it has only been in the last twenty years or so that professional teams began providing oxygen for their players. The reason they do that is to give them lungpower. A ready supply of oxygen on the sidelines is necessary to help them catch their breath so they'll be fresh when they get off the bench and get back in the game. This is also the reason for wind sprints in practice. Wind sprints build up the lungs capacity for oxygen. By expanding the lungs and exercising the heart, the body doesn't have to work as hard to undertake physical activity. It's part of being in shape. If you are going to preach, you too will need a ready supply of oxygen at your disposal. And the only way to maintain that supply is to practice mental discipline by exercising your body regularly.

It may surprise some of you more devout Bible believers; but, yes, this means that you will have to put on a pair of gym shorts and a tee-shirt possibly two or three times a week. It would be very hard to exercise wearing a three-piece suit and Oxford dress shoes with the little holes on the top. In fact, based on many of the preachers I've seen, this also means that a few gel and mouse hair dews will get messed up. But let me tell you, if you neglect to exercise that body God gave you, your congregation may end up burying you in that three-piece suit long before your time.

Exercise will not only keep you from getting overweight, but it will also help you not to become what I call a huffer or a gagger. These are preachers who tear along like a horse with a hornet in its ear until they run out of wind. That's when they must pause, take another breath to fill their lungs again and then keep running. You've heard the pause before. It's that guttural, gasping, grotesque, gesture of "ughhh" or "ha" between every four or five word phrase. This process of preaching till you run out of wind and sucking for more air is an indecent repetition that, unfortunately, is not uncommon, in spite of the fact that it can be altogether most distasteful, unpleasant, and painful to the ears.

Such preaching is evidence that many preachers have a misconception when it comes to using their voice. That's why I want to make this point very clear: it is not the loudness in your voice that makes it effective, it is the force that you put into your voice that makes it effective. You should never start out using the highest pitch within your voice range. When, or if, you do, there is no place else to ascend to. You have already started out as high as you can go. Instead, you should practice what is called in music, the crescendo. Crescendo is a

term used to describe a steady increase in volume. It serves to
gradually build the piece up to the high point of the song. The
same should apply to preaching. The high point is something
that you should work up to gradually.

If someone had tried to point this out to me many years
ago, I would have thought they were just trying to control my
preaching. I hope you won't make the same mistake. I'm
trying to tell you an effective way of speaking to be heard. I
can't make you listen. I can only offer to you what almost
thirty years of preaching has made clear to me. Effective
preaching isn't about volume, it's about being heard.

Don't wind up like so many preachers I've seen. Preachers
that thought they knew everything. Be wise. Protect your
voice. Don't ruin your throat and possibly end up with throat
cancer. Your voice and throat are the only tools besides the
scriptures that you have if you want to continue as a preacher.
It all ties back into using good common sense. The prepared
voice is the voice that is <u>protected</u> and <u>physically fit</u> so that it
can maintain a <u>proper pace</u> throughout the sermon. It is
developed through a lifestyle of discipline and also over years
of practice.

The Practiced Voice

Only through practice will you learn to moderate and
control what I refer to as "lung force." Lung force is essential
in moderating your tones and altering your pitch. This force
stems from the prepared voice that knows how to breathe. In
time, the practiced voice becomes very effective and dynamic.
It cannot remain one-dimensional. Instead, the practiced voice
will incorporate a variety of sounds capable of captivating the
attention of the hearers.

To harness the full potential of your speaking voice, you
should practice altering and varying its pitch frequently and
often. For example, when you preach, you should let the bass,
the treble, and the tenor parts of your voice each have their
turn in your address. When it comes to using your voice, don't

seek to be great – seek to be useful. It is through practice that you will develop your own unique style.

Practicing fluctuation in your delivery provides benefits over the long run as well. First, you get to keep your voice, and second, God can use you more productively. Think about it this way. If a drummer hits a drum in the same place every time he plays, it will not take long before the top skin wears out. Eventually, he will wear a hole through it. But if the drummer strikes the drumhead in different places to get different sounds, the skin of the head will last longer and it will be more useful in the long run. So it is with the voice of a preacher. If he is always using the same volume and the same pitch, it will eventually wear a hole in his throat. Moreover, the effectiveness produced by the alteration of words will also be lost forever. And like any other part of the body, once you lose the voice box, you can't get it back. It is like a soul. You only get one in a lifetime.

Practice and experience will teach you what suits your voice best. But, as I told you before, everything must be natural. Do not attempt to imitate another preacher's voice. Don't be an imitating monkey. Be a man. You are not a parrot. You are called to be a preacher. Use the voice God gave you. Practice with it. Learn its range. Experiment with it using variety and originality. It is your voice. Master it so that it can be useful for the Master.

The Protected Voice

There is nothing wrong with taking a few precautions to protect your voice. For example, during a preaching engagement, I suggest that you put on a coat, or a heavy shirt, to keep your body warm, even in the summer time. The last thing you need is to catch a cold and not be able to fulfill your commitment to preach at the meeting. I know that some preachers and evangelists can overplay this kind of thing, but it is still a good practice to follow.

Now some have suggested that preachers should use things like hard candy, throat lozenges, peppermints, etc. to keep their throats clear during a meeting. I personally don't recommend those things. I suggest that you keep away from all that sugar in your mouth while you're preaching a message. Its one thing for a horse to froth at the mouth during or after a race, but when a preacher on the platform has froth hanging off his lips during his delivery it is a pathetic sight. Learn to control your delivery so that your throat doesn't get too sore.

I suggest using cayenne pepper. You should not use any more than your stomach can stand. Don't overdo it and end up getting an upset stomach. You have to keep both your belly and your throat in good shape to deliver a message. Whenever my throat feels a little sore after a meeting, I prefer a good hot cup of tea, preferably green tea with honey and lemon. Usually it will clear up my throat by the next morning.

Never do what has been referred to as *preaching through* until your voice opens once again. That is a good way to damage your throat so that it takes longer to heal. If you are preaching the right way, you shouldn't be experiencing this kind of thing. Although I must admit that at times we can all get a little carried away with ourselves in the pulpit.

Remember that a sermon of nonsense is not made better simply because it is bellowed out of the pulpit. God never demanded that we shout at thirty or forty people inside our church building as though we were preaching to a stadium of ten thousand. George Whitefield said, "We use the language of the market." I would like to add to that statement. The greatest master of preaching is the man who is able to address any class of people in the manner suitable to their condition. Only then shall we be likely to touch their hearts.

The Prayerful Voice

The voice that a congregation hears in public must be a voice that God has already heard in private. This is an essential point to remember in your delivery, especially if you intend to touch the souls of the men and women listening. This will help you once the preaching gets underway so that you can know by experience where Adam leaves you and where the Spirit of God leads you. It has been said that where the sun does not enter the doctor soon follows. Well said. For when the preacher, through his own undeveloped gift, fails to bring forth Jesus and let Him shine, then souls become ill very fast. To keep this from happening in your pulpit, heed the words of the great preachers from days gone by. Adam Clark said it like this:

> Study yourself to death, then pray yourself alive, then address the congregation afresh from on high, and feed the hungry souls with manna from above and conviction to the lost sinners!

Or, John Wesley, when he said:

> Thy soul must overflow, if thou another's soul would reach,
> It needs the overflow of heart, to give the lips full speech.

Elijah said: **"and the God that answereth by fire, let him be God"** (1 Kings 18:24). The man whose tongue is on fire for God, let him be God's minister. Over the years, I've noticed that young men with a calling upon their lives have a tendency to feed their brain instead of their heart. This ought not to be so. It seems that in our day and age most young men are so caught up with impressing their mentors that they dig too deep and they surely come up dry, very dry, in their delivery. Many Bible schools, institutes, colleges, and seminaries have gathered much fuel, but they have surely lost the fire with which to kindle it.

Speaking from the Heart

An effective delivery requires more than just a preacher's voice. It demands a preacher's heart. It must be a heart on fire for the Lord; a heart full of passion and zeal. Elijah found out that God will indeed answer by fire. We, as preachers, must feed the flames. They need fuel or else the lamp of God will go out in the sanctuary. Consider the words of Dylan Thomas: "You cannot go away gently, you must rage against the dying of the light."[2]

As preachers, we should not go away gently. We should rage against the sinfulness of men that seeks to extinguish the Light of the world from our presence. Our zeal must be displayed. Our earnestness in the pulpit must be real. It cannot be mimicked. It should never be counterfeited. Nothing but the truth of the Word can be blessed in the house of the Lord.

Be earnest and zealous in your delivery. Don't give any mind to those who try to dampen the fires of the pulpit with their melancholy discourse of the scriptures. Let your zeal and sincerity abound. A burning heart will soon find for itself a flaming tongue. Never shame those who are earnest and zealous in the pulpit. Don't let the desire to court popularity and prestige entice you to fall to such a contemptible level. Abhor the very thought of ever doing so. Forsake the dullard preachers that speak ever so kindly with regard to sin and ever so critical with regard to God's word. Leave them to their own anemic pulpits filled with their monotonous voices. They are the ones who pour water on the fires of earnestness and zeal that burn within the hearts of those who desire truth and a closer fellowship with the Lord Jesus Christ. It would be infinitely better that such preachers would make their ministries a masquerade and themselves actors. If you must choose between zeal and knowledge, take the zeal every time.

I'm convinced that no man who preaches the gospel without zeal is sent from God. Such a man is not a preacher at all. I've preached in the South for over twenty-three years. In that time I've noticed that most preaching is like fiddle playing. People come to see how well you can do it. Once they hear you, they start passing around the question, "What did you think of him?" That, my fellow preachers, is not the main question we should concern ourselves with as preachers. I'll tell you what we should care about. Care about the fact that there is a whole world dying and on its way to Hell. Care about what a man thinks of Christ. And care about what people think concerning their eternal state.

The gospel of our Lord Jesus Christ is what we must care about and stand for. So let's stand to our preaching like Marines to their weapons. Let our pulpits be the firebases of Christianity. They should be like the battlefield of Khe-Sanh in Vietnam; a place where the enemy tasted defeat. Let us preach and preach evermore my brethren. Preach the gospel until it shakes the gates of Hell and souls are eternally set free. Preach the gospel until prodigals return home. This is our Master's mandate and the Master's power is given to all who will believe. Life, death, Hell, and worlds unknown are hanging on the preaching of our sermons.

The preaching of sermons is what we are about. We are preachers. Yes. We do preach, but that is not just something that we do – it is something that we are. It's like Michael Angelo said, "It is only well with me when I have my chisel in my hand." I'll be honest with you. It is only well with me when I can preach.

We must all work at perfecting our delivery so that we speak from the heart. We have adult men here at Blue Ridge Bible Institute in our preaching class. When they are preaching, I watch them and the way that they conduct themselves. As I said before, I have been studying preachers and preaching for many years. So, I watch for their most outstanding idiosyncrasies. I've found that when they are corrected about a particular defect, they have a tendency to protect their feelings instead of trying to perfect their pulpit gift. Preaching from the heart does not mean that you should be overly sensitive.

Unfortunately, the worst kind of preaching takes place in front of people. Once it goes out, you can't pull it back in. If you have the wrong spirit when you preach, this will do damage to the hearers. You shouldn't be preaching just to rant and rave and put people down. The end result should be to pick people up and pull them out of the fire. That requires you to have the right kind of heart, a heart that is in tune with God. Preach to people the right way. Have the right kind of spirit and the right motive. That is the only kind of preaching worth listening to. That doesn't mean you trade your Sword for a butter knife. Preachers who do not aim to cut deep into the hearts of men are not worth their salt. So when delivering a message, be yourself, but make sure you have the right spirit about you. The true *you* will come out in the process of time when God believes that you're ready.

If we want to touch the hearts of listeners, then the messages must come from our hearts first. It has been a long time since I preached a sermon that I was satisfied with. I scarcely recollect ever having done so. The body of Christ has become professional with regard to preaching. We preach like robots that are wound up for a sermon and timed to run down when the message is over.

Dr. Noe once said that a preacher should saturate his sermons with Bible and the essence of Bible truths so that he will always have something new to say. But just because you give your listeners something new, don't make it too hard for them to understand. Many preachers cause their congregations to work on Sunday. Their messages are so unclear that the listeners must do hard labor in order to decipher through the terrible delivery. They must rack their souls instead of resting them in order to comprehend what is being said.

We should be intent on announcing the truth more so than convincing men of the truth. Even Paul did not consider himself to be a *persuader* in terms of the rhetoric of his day. His duty, like ours, was to announce. When we are delivering our messages for God we are nothing more than the mouthpiece. Anything that hinders the truth of the text being delivered must be divorced immediately. In fact, it should be broken off even before the vows are made. Engage the listeners so that the truth of the text you are delivering comes across clear and passionately.

Style of Delivery

Now when we talk about the style of the delivery, we all have different ones that we like or feel more comfortable with. Over the years I've found that preacher's gifts are all different. Our presentation styles are different as well.

Olford again provides valuable insight:

> On the practical level, the preacher should seek to preach in such a way that he deserves the attention of the audience. This is not to say that attention will always be given, but the preacher's message and delivery should call for attention.[3]

It is our job to help the audience become attentive to the truth that we are proclaiming. So the following are a few common sense points about delivering a message that will enable you to reach this objective:

- Apply the truths of the message to everyday life.
- Keep focused on the subject you are dealing with.
- Speak from the heart.
- Avoid addressing petty and superficial things in your delivery.[4]

Paul gave Timothy a few practical pieces of instruction about preaching. And by the way, Timothy followed and ministered to Paul for ten years before he ever became the pastor over the church of the Ephesians. Here is what Paul said:

- Recognize the gift; **"the gift of God, which is in thee…"** (2 Timothy 1:6)
- Maximize the gift; **"neglect not the gift that is in thee…"**   (1 Timothy 4:14)

- Utilize the gift; **"stir up the gift of God, which is in thee…"** (2 Timothy 1:6)[5]

It has been said that you cannot separate the man and his message. That is absolutely correct. God must not only be working through the message, but through the man as well. Use your God given abilities. Then know and understand the scriptural truths about delivery.

It doesn't matter that you've been saved for a couple of years now or that you've heard preaching and read every commentary recommended by the Bible believing crowd. Brothers, according to that book you profess to believe in, there is something more important to consider. You need to first take a look at what the Bible says and then take heed to it long before you go out to set the world on fire.

I had a young man come to me one time who, I must admit, seemed to have a calling upon his life. Although at that time he was still in what I considered an embryonic stage as far as preaching was concerned. He said that he had about five to eight people who wanted to start a church. He then informed me that he had been called to pastor. What did I do? I handed him a pack of matches and said, "Very well, if God is in it, go for it. But, if He isn't, you better first do the two things that Paul talked about in 1 Corinthians before you do anything else." My advice is the same to you. Here it is:

#1 – Master the Delivery of a Message (1 Corinthians 2:1) **"Declaring unto you the testimony of God."** You have to know the message before you can proclaim it. Proclaiming a message is not a performance. There is too much pressure in Bible schools today to perform. Preaching isn't simply a performance. I believe it would be better for young men who've been called by God to preach (which would include everything from pastors to missionaries) to go and sit under someone who has been in the ministry for at least fifteen years. They could learn a few valuable lessons such as how to minister and how NOT to quit. The novices could learn by first hand experience the things to do and the things not to do as a minister of God, which would include all aspects of the calling mentioned throughout in this writing.

#2 – Master the Ways to Deliver a Message (1 Corinthians 2:4):

And my speech and my preaching was not with enticing words of man's wisdom, but in demonstration of the Spirit and of power.

Many preachers do more damage to the cause of Christ by running into the battle severely under-equipped than they would have if they had only taken some time to learn a few things beforehand.   One area that preachers need to learn about is the realm of the supernatural. What I'm saying is that a supernatural encounter must take place in a man's life long before that man's ministry will ever be effective. This kind of thing moves well into a realm where most preachers have never walked nor ever will.   That's because a man's ego and pride is not allowed to tread upon this holy ground of preparation.

Spurgeon said, "Where the application begins, there the delivery of the sermon begins."[6] This means that in order for the message to be applied, you must make it clear and plain. The plainer it is the better it is.

Our delivery should be aimed at getting a spiritual response from the congregation.   Make the points logical, easy to understand, and comprehensible. Those are all components of a good delivery.   Here is an acronym that will help you to keep these points about effective delivery in mind:

Devoutly prepared.
Earnestly entreated.
Lovingly applied.
Impartially addressed.
Verbally understood.

Epitaphic in its goal.
Relentless in its address.
Yoked with the truth.

When this common sense approach combines with the supernatural presence of the Holy Spirit, effective preaching can occur. Effectively gaining a response from the hearers is what we are aiming at in our delivery. Also remember to keep bad habits out of the pulpit, such as nervous ticks, swaying, or staring people down. You should also avoid things such as pounding on the Bible, ripping it up, kicking it, or cleaning glasses with the pages of it. People hold the word of God in reverence. We should do the same in the pulpit. And never patronize well-known preachers in a meeting by mentioning their names over and over again in your address. The people are watching you.

Therefore, demonstrate a balance in the visual area as well as in the vocal area. Throughout the delivery, be aware of who you are, whose you are, and what you are doing. You are delivering a sermon as a message from God.

May the mind of Christ, my Saviour, live in me from day to day,
By His love and power controlling, all I do and say.
May the Word of God dwell richly, in my heart from hour to hour,
So that all may see I triumph, only through His power.
May the peace of God, my Father, rule my life in everything,
that I may claim a comfort, to the sick and sorrowing.
May the love of Jesus fill me, as waters fill the sea,
Him exalting, self-abasing, This is victory.
May I run the race before me, strong and brave to face the foe,
Looking only unto Jesus, as I onward go.
May His beauty rest upon me, as I seek the lost to win,
And may they forget the channel, seeing only Him.
Kate B. Wilkinson[7]

When it comes to preaching, that poem sums it up well. To be an effective old path preacher, you will need to get out of the way, let go, and let God. All we can do is to get prayed up, studied up, and then standby to see what God will do in our messages. Our prayer should be that He will bless His word and use us as a voice crying in the wilderness, **"Prepare ye the way of the Lord"** (Isaiah 40:3).

12

Proper Timing in the Delivery

Proper timing is another very important aspect of delivering an effective message from the word of God. In fact, timing is relative to practically every aspect of life. It is of the utmost importance. Did you ever stop to consider that there is an entire chapter in the Bible dedicated to this important subject? The entire third chapter of the book of Ecclesiastes is dedicated to the realm of time.

We obviously recognize the importance of timing in other pursuits aside from preaching. Take sports for an example. In football, there is nothing more exciting than the perfect pass thrown way downfield to the receiver - the Bomb. It can be even more exciting when time is running out and it's fourth down and long. The ball is snapped. The quarterback drops back in the pocket and releases the pass in the midst of a defensive rush. The ball sails sixty yards downfield. The wide receiver glances over his shoulder just in time to fully extend his body in mid-air so that the ball falls perfectly into his outstretched hands only inches away from the defender's effort to deflect and within a shoestring of being out of bounds of the goal line. Touchdown! What makes a play like that so exciting and thrilling? Timing. It's all about timing

There is also the timing that comes with the hike of the ball, the handoff, and the perfectly timed block or tackle. Football is a game filled with timing. It involves movement and speed. The same applies to other sports as well. In baseball, there is the speed of the pitch. Timing determines whether the batter's swing knocks the ball out of the park or strikes him out. In basketball, there is the head fake of the center before a drive to the basket for a slam-dunk or the behind-the-back pass of the guard following the fast break that leads to a score. Both moves involve precision and timing. In boxing, the speed and combination of punches determines the champion. If not for good timing, nobody would be interested in watching sports. Timing is essential even in the business world. A good entrepreneur must know when to buy, sell, or hold if he hopes to remain a going concern for very long. Timing impacts almost every facet of our daily lives.

With regard to preaching, timing is the key that will unlock and open the ears of the congregation. If that statement is true (and it is), then a preacher should seek to grasp the essentials of good timing in his message as though he were struggling for his last breath of air upon the earth. Timing is so important, not only because it brings the listener into the message, but also because it can keep them there. To capture the listener's ear, the preacher must be a) demonstrative – use timing to illustrate the point being made, b) deliberate – intentionally use timing for its effect, and c) judicial – capable of discerning the appropriate moment of time and then knowing what to do.

These abilities can only be learned from experience. Experience is the only teacher in the classroom of oratorical ability and skill. In this area, practice does not always make perfect. Poor timing can become a permanent flaw if you don't know how to use it to your advantage. One must know when to speak up, when to cool down, when to scream something to get attention, and when to bring things down to a guttural growl so that you can keep the crowd's attention or make a point. A sense of timing is necessary so that you can know when to give an invitation and when not to, how long to keep it going and when to shut it down. As we have already discussed, the opening and the closing are vitally important parts of an effective message. You have to know when to throw and how to throw the gospel net. And it all comes down to timing.

In terms of preaching, I honestly believe that it is a dying art. Not for the lack of good material, but the lack of good timing and proper delivery. Too many preachers want to give people an in depth sermon that ends up being an in-length delivery instead. Messages today usually lack simplicity. As preachers, we need to remember that eloquence is contingent upon simplicity. We must learn to be concise in our speech and get to the point. Long messages may be pleasant when we are doing the speaking, but for the listeners, they can be the utmost torture. The long-winded sermon can also be a sign of the preacher's ignorance. A preacher without a sense of timing is like a horse without a bridle. He goes nowhere, lacks direction, and is of little use. In this day and time, the body of Christ needs the elegant style of old-time biblical preaching that involves simplicity, brevity, and last but not least, good timing. Good timing will help to hold people's attention. It is a critical component of an effective old path preaching style.

A young preacher approached me one evening after a church service. He wanted to know more about how to keep the people's attention when he preached. He asked me to tell him how. I asked him how long he had been preaching. He said he had been preaching for a few years in rest homes, jails, and occasionally in church. I answered him in one word – experience.

"But what about those men who have preached for many years and still fail to keep people's attention," he asked. My reply was this – "It's all about timing." I told him that developing a proper use of timing would help his messages make a chief impression upon the hearers. Almost everybody has ears. With enough experience, you can learn to tickle those ears. That is another skill developed by the proper use of timing.

With practice, a preacher can learn to use the skill of good timing to catch the listener's judgment in order to show them what kind of person they are through the light of the Word. It involves and requires the use of good timing throughout the delivery of the sermon.

With these points in mind, let's make a short overview of timing as it applies to the introduction, the message, the closing, and the invitation.

Timing in the Introduction

As we have already made clear, the introduction, or opening, is a very important part of the message. It is at this point that we can either capture or lose the hearers. So, in order to put the listeners at ease, many preachers start off here with a joke, a poem, or a short story. Whatever you choose to do, be ready to step into the pulpit and deliver. Take it seriously, but don't be rigid and tense. If you are prepared and prayed up, you will eventually develop what I call a pulpit presence. I'm not talking about a presence where you strut around carrying your Bible under you arm like a perched buzzard waiting for another piece of food. A pulpit presence is a spiritual and supernatural presence. This is missing in about 99% of pulpits today, but it didn't use to be like that. It used to be that when God's man entered the pulpit, things changed. The atmosphere became different. People knew the preacher had arrived. It is rarely like that anymore. However, I have seen it happen.

I specifically recall an occasion when I went to hear Bro. Lester Roloff preach. Before he arrived that morning the place was already packed out. Everyone was standing around talking and greeting each other when all of a sudden I felt a change in the building. The atmosphere became different although most people just kept on talking. That's when I turned around and saw preacher Roloff entering the building. He had something on him and it was strong. It was heavenly and powerful. He was a humble man, but he definitely had a pulpit presence.

Personally, I like to start out by reading the text and then asking someone to pray and bless the reading. While that brother is praying, I have a minute to set the timing for the opening. I'll tell myself, "Jim, it's time to get the cart in gear and grab their attention." So when he finishes praying, I usually say in a growl. "This is one of the greatest passages found in the Bible."

Start off the introduction by giving a doctrinal application of the passage. This is a good practice that will keep the rest of the message from being misunderstood with regards to how it fits doctrinally and to whom it applies. Then you can start to explain the passage. Use your voice to get their attention. I like to bring mine to a crescendo at this part of the delivery and then level off as I call their attention to the text and look at the practical application. At this point, timing can be important. If I'm before an audience of Northerners, I might say, "Let's look at this passage and see what God can show us today." If the people are from the South, I'll change up the words a bit by saying, "Let's look at this passage and see what learning we can get from it today." Timing is involved here.

The opening should be no more than four to five minutes long at the most. Remember, the attention of the listeners must be gained at this point or you won't get anything accomplished. In homiletics, this is called the crucial five minutes. This is the place where you either gain or loose the attention of the listeners. Remember, if your opening fails to gain the ears of those who are listening, then the sermon that follows will be sure to lose their attention. When Napoleon fought against the Austrians, he said that his success was given to the first five minutes of the battle. There's an old country saying that's good to keep in mind when it comes to the introduction: "Well begun is half done."

You can do all the word spinning you want, but if the people's attention is not gained, nothing eternal will come out of it. If men's minds are not grabbed and captivated by the opening, then their minds will start to wander and they will not receive the truth set before them. Sin cannot be taken out of men, as Eve was taken out of Adam, while they sleep! We must awaken our congregations, so that they can understand what we are presenting to them in the opening portion of our sermons. They need to hear and feel the force or they will more than likely fall asleep.

This requires you from the very onset to give the listeners something that they can treasure up and remember. Make it something useful to them. Give them manna. Let them begin to smell the hot manna from God as the skies begin to open from above.

Make this a rule. Do not let the opening go too long, never past five minutes. It is always a shame to see a great porch built on the front of a little house. The only thing that tells us is that the builder didn't have much sense about how to put things together. The same applies to preachers who don't know how to put the right opening on their messages and fail to hold people's attention. The only thing that a sermon builder will receive is criticism about the way things were put together. Unfortunately, many sermons are exactly like that.

So here is what an effective opening should accomplish:

- it should lead the listeners directly into the message
- it should never promise more than what the sermon can deliver
- it should be simple, short, and informative
- it should use variety; beware of ritualism and also *rut*-ualism (The only difference between a rut and a grave is the depth.)
- never be longer than four to five minutes. A long opening inevitably becomes tiresome to the listeners and it defeats the main purpose, which is to awaken the attention of the listeners, not to exhaust their patience.

Socrates said, "I have spent my entire life bringing people from a state of unconscious ignorance to a condition of conscious ignorance." It will take about twenty years of preaching to fully understand that saying.

Timing in the Message

You must always understand that the message is much more important than the messenger. Many preachers have said that their messages changed thousands of lives. I say, no sir, they have not! Only the word of God works to change lives, not a man's message. Many preachers have had good outlines, and if God had been in them, they would have been grand messages.

In my messages, I like to use the system called alliteration, which is the repetitious use of the same letter at the beginning of the main points of the sermon. Examples of this outline style are provided in the appendix. Although there is not an established rule that must be followed, I personally believe that this style of presentation helps you to maintain your thought and keep the listener's attention. It may be necessary for you to get a good thesaurus so that you have an easy resource for synonyms and antonyms. I recommend the thesaurus as a required tool if you intend to follow this system.

Alliteration also indicates that you have put some thought into the sermon instead of the normal, "Glad I'm saved! Glad I'm saved! Glad I'm saved! Glad you're saved! Glad you're saved! Yes, glad you're saved! We need to get'em saved! Oh yes, we need to get'em saved!"

I recently heard from one of our former students. He told me about a message that he had heard entitled, "How to Keep a Good Pastor." The points went something like this: Pray for Him, Stay for Him, Pay for Him and Say for Him (I suppose that means witness). The four-point poem went like this: Pray-Stay-Pay-Say. That is not the kind of message I am proposing here. Unfortunately, these kinds of sermons are being blurted out all over the country. Since they don't affect the listeners in their sin, churches have grown accustomed to hearing these un-biblical messages brought to them on serving trays of financial advancement. The waiters in this self-proclaimed service aren't worried about whether the word of God impacts the hearers. They're just waiting for a tip for their service.

If you are going to use the alliteration style, it must come naturally for you. Once again, experience plays a role here. Preaching your message correctly will require you to learn how to pause. A good pause secures the attention of the listeners. Pull up short every once in the while so that the sleepers on the train wake up. The pause cannot be too long or overly extended. If it is, then the listeners will think you're stumbling or reading because of being unstudied. Overextending will cause you to lose the very thing you seek to gain – their attention.

I'll say it again. Alliteration is not something that can be taught by an instructor. It is one of the fancies of preaching that a man can only learn by experience. Trial and error are the best teachers in this area. Pause – then give them a common sense golden one-liner to set the gospel nail into their heart. If you never learn to touch the heart, be assured that the ears will soon become weary to your delivery.

In preaching, there is an element of delivery in every God called preacher. Gentlemen, saturate your sermons with the word of God and let it feed the hungry. In everything be natural, lest you be discovered as an imposter of someone else that they have listened to. Stay away from sounding like another preacher. Learn only to emulate the excellence of grand orators. Learn the how to's and the how not to's. Through it all, strive to implement good timing. The message drives home only if we follow the avenue of timing. Without timing, the message is nothing more than a common, dull, and boring dissertation. Good timing may appear difficult to attain at first. But it will eventually form and prove to be beneficial as a man continually develops this aspect of his preaching.

With preaching, we never reach a plateau of excellence. The longer that I'm saved and continue to preach the riches of

His grace, the more I see within myself the need to strive for excellence; the more I recognize my lack of preaching skills. Oh, how I want to be a vessel for my Lord – just a voice in the wilderness.

Timing in the Closing

This is the part of the message where all things wind up. In every message all roads lead to this place. Here is where the listeners have been brought (we hope) to a decision. If you wish to preach with effect then the first two parts of timing (timing in the introduction and timing in the message) are extremely important, but this third part is of uttermost importance. Good timing in the closing means knowing when to quit. You must develop a feel for it in order to do this part right. Even a washing machine knows it's time to quit when the water runs out. And don't commit the sin of Baptist preachers by saying, "one more thing" only to follow up with four or five more things. Remember to "Get Up – Speak Up – and then Shut Up." Or, as we gentlemen say down home here in Carolina, "HUSH!!!"

Sometimes you may not get through your whole outline. Sometimes God moves before you expect or plan. He wants to do business. Again, this is something that you can only learn by experience. It cannot be taught. But if you never learn this then you will not catch too many in the gospel net.

Timing in the Invitation

I suppose that I've seen more misuse in this part of the message that any other, especially when it comes to timing. I've watched as some preachers just let the sinners go and then others refuse to let anybody go. Singing twenty-four stanzas of "Just As I Am" is too much and it won't get you any results.

Learn to get a feel for this part of the sermon. It is of the utmost importance. I used to watch the older preachers give invitations. Harold Sightler was a good one. I studied him many times to see how he reached the point of decision. I listened and watched his voice, his body language, and where he directed his attention. He was good at bringing people to the point of a decision. To be an old path preacher, you must know how to throw the net. I've watched a lot of them.

Dr. Noe, Maze Jackson, Jack Wood, Percy Ray, Sammy Allen, Don Greene, Ed Ballew, Jack Hyles, Lester Roloff, John Rawlings, G.B.Vick, Tom Malone and many other camp meeting preachers. They were all good. But in my opinion the best net thrower was Dr. Lackey. He was an old-fashioned country preacher, and most people don't know how well studied he was when it came to the Bible. That man had a supernatural gift from God. He knew how to throw the net to catch sinners, whether lost or saved. He could reel them back to God.

I wish I could put it into words all that this man taught me in the area of timing. I asked him many times how to and when to. He would just smile and say, "Watch, Red." He would preach for about an hour on everything under the sun from chewing bubble gum in church to how tight a woman's britches were. He would make people mad. I mean really mad and irate. Then, he would get ready, throw the net, and the sinners would come. He had the gift. It was by all means supernatural.

When I first started out, many of the older preachers were looking for young men to follow them. I shunned away from that crowd. Preacher Lackey was different. I had the opportunity to ride with him one time to Houston, TX on his bus. He talked with me all the way there. I wish to this day that I had taken a tape recorder so that I could refer back to his wisdom. When he asked me what I wanted, I said, "I want to learn how to throw the net, preacher."

I remember the last time I saw Dr. Lackey. I preached at his church on his birthday. He was sitting on the platform in a rocker. He told me, "Judgment boy, preach judgment Red!" When the sermon ended I looked over at him. The Lord was moving in the invitation. He just smiled at me with that upside down smile. I realized that I had learned something important from that man – timing. Good timing can make all the difference in the invitation. I can't stress the point enough. Timing is of the uttermost importance in every area of a message.

After that day I never saw Dr. Lackey again. I know I'll see him again in Glory and I'll be able to thank him for his unmerited attention toward me. To this day, every time I preach, I see two things in my mind. First, I see my own Mother. Much to my regret and disappointment, she died a sinner's death back in 1978. Before she left us she came to an Easter Cantata at a church we were attending. She had never been in a Baptist church before. Afterwards, we went out to eat. She said, "Jimmy, next time you preach, Mama's going to come hear you. Look for me honey, I'll be in the back pew." She left us before I ever had that next opportunity to preach with her there in the congregation. Lucifer has sure been consistent since that time. He always calls my attention to the back row every time I preach, whether in my church or some other place. Then he'll say to me, "If God is so good, why is she in Hell?"

Second, I see an old man with white hair. He's looking at me again with his upside down smile. I can hear him saying, "Watch, Red." Sometimes I can still hear that old North Carolina drawl giving me encouragement from behind saying, "You got it, Red."

13

Heretical vs. Biblical Leadership

I do not claim to be an expert on any subject, especially when it comes to leadership. In fact, I'd say that the only thing that I have truly mastered here on this earth is sinning. I don't say that proudly, but with much shame. But as I begin this chapter, I want to discuss what I believe to be a very real problem in churches today – the absence of leadership. What is prevalent in many churches today is not leadership at all, but a perversion of it. In most cases, it can only be described as a dictatorship or on the other hand, some sort of a puppet show. Neither one is true leadership; yet, both are heretical in nature because they contradict the teachings of the Bible. As a Baptist preacher, and also as a man who believes the word of God, I'm compelled to expose these two fallacies so that we can then learn the scriptural approach to leadership based solely on the Bible. Being the right kind of leader is essential if you expect people to follow you down the old paths.

The Dictatorship

Dictatorships are very prevalent within the body of Christ today. I don't know why there are so many pastors out there who feel that it is necessary for them to oversee every detail in the lives of their church members. I suppose that these men are so insecure that they feel the need to control everything around them in order to get their own way. They have a Nicolaitan mentality. That is a mindset that seeks to conquer other people and to lord over them. These are pastors who are afflicted with the "big me, little you" syndrome.

The dictator-styled pastor wants to make every decision affecting the lives of his church members whether large or small. For example, whether or not you can get married, the person you marry, the clothes that you wear, what you think, what you look at, what you possess in your home, and the list goes on and on. There seems to be no end to all they seek to control in the lives of others. The dictator-pastor strives to maintain the role of Master within their own universe as well as set themselves up as the final authority in the lives of those around them.

In their view, you, as their church member, have no mind of your own. You are only allowed to think, believe, and act in a manner that they think is right and approve of. If not, they consider you to be "out of fellowship" or "not right with God." I don't know exactly what that is, but I do know that it isn't leadership. It does fall well within the realm of foolishness. And the old saying applies here, "No one is thinking if everyone is thinking alike."[1]

In churches run by dictators, you are sure to find what I call puppy dog men as the deacons and officers. They are the "yes" men, but they are definitely not real men who love God. I say that because such men are not worshipping God, instead, they are worshipping a preacher. And dictators rely on these kinds of individuals to support them. Their survival depends on it. However, that kind of setup should never be considered leadership.

Dictators need people around them who don't read their Bibles so they can easily fool them. In that environment, they can boast of their theological degrees and appear to be a spiritual authority. Remember this, the more praise a man is willing to receive, the less he deserves. Such preachers enjoy bragging on their accomplishments or maybe even their membership roles as proof that God is "blessing." Besides, they have a following. Listen, the Rev. Jim Jones had followers. So, what did that prove? That is not the basis for demanding respect and requiring people to follow you.

Dictators operate under the false assumption that their position demands the respect of others because of a title. However, they fail to realize that respect is not a commodity that can be purchased with a title or a position, or even a pocketbook. Respect must first be established upon character.

You see, a man can borrow brains, but he cannot borrow character. Although your brains may get you a theological degree that leads to a position of authority in a church, it doesn't mean that you've earned respect. Respect only comes after years of biblically based service in the ministry. Respect and authority are not the birthrights of men who hold the title of Dr., PhD, or any other theological degree.

Dictators are leprous spots. They infect churches, ruin people's lives, and enslave the body of Christ. The danger is that so many Christian people accept them and consider the bondage that these men put them under as a normal part of Christianity. With their magisterial and popish form of control, these dictators force their vain rules and regulations upon those in their flocks and call it ministry when, in fact, it is nothing more than madness.

The Puppet Show

The other extreme on the spectrum of leadership so-called is what I refer to as the *puppet-show*. Puppet show preachers operate on strings. Every move they make is controlled by someone in their congregation, but not by God. The puppet show preacher is typically managed by the head deacon, the board of deacons, the family that established the church back in 1800, the wealthiest church members, or some other influential person on the church role. Whoever is running the show, one thing is for certain, it isn't the preacher and it surely isn't God.

In this scenario, the preacher serves as nothing more than a hired employee. He has no say in the business of the church. He must preach from on top of the breadbox lest he fall off, or get shoved off, and thus starve himself and his family. This is not preaching and it certainly isn't leadership. And it is about as biblical as the pope of Rome being referred to as the "Vicar of Christ."

There is no need to expound in detail on this kind of situation. We only need to recognize it for what it is and for what it is not. With that said, let's move on to examine the offices of leadership within the local church.

Biblical Leadership

In Ephesians 4:11, the Bible names five gifts given to the church:

> **And he gave some, apostles; and some, prophets; and some, evangelists; and some, pastors and teachers;**

In this verse, Paul refers back to the gifts that were given to men by the Lord Jesus Christ following his ascension as mentioned in Ephesians 4:8:

> **8) Wherefore he saith, When he ascended up on high, he led captivity captive, and gave gifts unto men.**
> **9) Now that he ascended, what is it but that he also descended first into the lower parts of the earth?**

These verses make it clear that apostles, prophets, evangelists, pastors and teachers were and are New Testament gifts from the Lord to the body of Christ. These gifts were given after Christ ascended back to heaven. With the coming of the Holy Ghost in Acts 2, gifts were given unto men. These gifts are not signs (i.e., "tongues, miracles, healings"). Keeping within the context of the passage, we know from verse eleven that the gifts given unto men are the offices of apostle, prophet, evangelist, pastor and teacher. Let's briefly look at each of these.

Apostles/Prophets

The first ten chapters of the book of Acts establish the fact that apostles were necessary in the early formation of the Christian church. They confirmed the word of God with signs following (Mark 16:20). Keep in mind that at this point in history the New Testament canon was not yet complete. Also, there were more New Testament apostles than just the twelve that walked with the Lord during His earthly ministry. Some of the other apostles mentioned in the Bible include: Silas, Paul, Junia, Apollos, Timothy, Sosthenes, and Barnabas. As the body of Christ began to grow, prophets appeared throughout the remainder of Acts (see chapters 11-28). They were necessary as the church began to mature. Following the time period of the book of Acts, three of the gifts given to men have prevailed: evangelists, pastors and teachers.

Evangelists

An evangelist is a rare breed to say the least. When I say evangelist, I'm not talking about pastors who swap pulpits with other pastors, although a pastor is instructed to do the work of an evangelist. Evangelism is a specific gift given by God to certain men. With regard to evangelism, 2 Timothy 4:5 states:

But watch thou in all things, endure afflictions, do the work of an evangelist, make full proof of thy ministry.

A true evangelist is a man who helps local churches. He can encourage them by setting up citywide meetings, revivals, and other such gatherings. Today, most evangelistic work is not broad based over a particular city. Instead, it is centered upon the local church with meetings running over the span of three days to a week. Although some preachers still travel overseas to hold evangelistic meetings, only the most famous ones are known.

Looking back through church history, we can recognize the names of many great evangelists. To name them all would be too many to mention. But I can tell you who the last one in America was. Regardless of whether or not you agree, or whether you hate him or like him, it was without a doubt Billy Graham. He was the last great evangelist as far as national, worldwide evangelism is concerned. I realize that there may be many others today that I haven't heard of that are still out there traveling the roads, but Billy Graham was the last well-recognized evangelist.

One thing I do know about evangelism is that a man must have a direct calling from God to perform that office. As a matter of fact, nearly every Bible school graduate who thinks his calling is to be an evangelist usually discovers otherwise pretty quick, especially when God closes the door on him Personally, I will not let a man hold an evangelistic meeting in my church if he has never pastored a local church. That has been my practice for the past seventeen years here at Bridgeport Baptist Church. You may disagree. But after seeing and hearing evangelists who have never pastored a local church, and after seeing the mess they can make in some other pastor's church, I say, "No thank you." I can stir up enough hornets in the nest here by myself without any help from outside.

By the way, a missionary on deputation is not an evangelist. I know that many of them like to mention their evangelistic labors in their newsletters, such as the number of meetings they have held and the revivals they have preached, but that doesn't mean that God called them to the ministry of evangelism. A missionary and an evangelist aren't the same thing.

The only evangelist that I know of personally who fills this office according to the biblical standard is Dr. Sam Gipp. He has a biblically based evangelistic ministry that can minister to and encourage a local church. That is the true calling of a man called to be an evangelist. I believe Dr. Gipp does the work of an evangelist the right way based on New Testament evangelistic principles.

Pastors and Teachers

From a chronological perspective, the final group identified as ministering to the body of Christ in the last days before the rapture is pastors and teachers. I want you to notice something in Ephesians 4:11: there is no comma between the word *pastor* and the word *teacher*. There's a reason for that. A pastor is not just a pastor. He is also supposed to be a teacher. Look at 2 Timothy 2:11, where Paul wrote,

> **Whereunto I am appointed a <u>preacher</u>, and an apostle, and a <u>teacher </u>of the Gentiles.**

Also observe 1 Timothy 3:2:

> **A bishop then must be blameless, the husband of one wife, vigilant, sober, of good behavior, given to hospitality, <u>apt to teach</u>;**

According to the Bible, a pastor must also be able to teach the members of his church. He must help them to learn the important doctrines of the Bible so that they will not be misled by the wrong teachers who are all to willing to scratch itching ears (2 Timothy 4:3). If you want to be a good under-shepherd, then you will have to become a good teacher. However, a good teacher must first be known as a good student. That's important. If you refuse to take the time to sit under the teaching of others and learn something yourself, then don't expect to have anything worthwhile to teach others and don't expect anybody to sit down and listen to you.

As you know, the role of a pastor is critical in the operation of the local church. Paul teaches us some things about the role of a pastor and his authority in this office. In Hebrews 13:7, the Bible says:

> **Remember them which have the rule over you, who have spoken unto you the word of God: whose faith follow, considering the end of their conversation.**

Then again, in Hebrews 13:17-25, we read:

> **17) Obey them that have the rule over you, and submit yourselves: for they watch for your souls, as they must give account, that they may do it with joy, and not with grief: for that is unprofitable for you.**
> **18) Pray for us: for we trust we have a good conscience, in all things willing to live honestly.**
> **19) But I beseech you the rather to do this, that I may be restored to you the sooner.**
> **20) Now the God of peace, that brought again from the dead our Lord Jesus, that great shepherd of the sheep, through the blood of the everlasting covenant,**
> **21) Make you perfect in every good work to do his will, working in you that which is well pleasing in his sight, through Jesus Christ; to whom be glory for ever and ever. Amen.**
> **22) And I beseech you, brethren, suffer the word of exhortation: for I have written a letter unto you in few words.**

23) Know ye that our brother Timothy is set at liberty; with whom, if he come shortly, I will see you.
24) Salute all them that have the rule over you, and all the saints. They of Italy salute you.
25) Grace be with you all. Amen."

These are two important passages addressing the role of the pastor in a church. They make it clear that within the local church, God established a system of authority. These verses provide sufficient evidence to show that there are those within the local church who are to hold positions of leadership. In fact, in Hebrews 13:24 (see above), the Bible says that we should *salute* those that have the rule over us. Do you know what it means to salute? A salute is a specific manner in which we honor a position. To salute, as we know it today in the military, started during medieval days. Whenever one knight saw another knight in full armor, they would lift their face shields to see who it was they were passing and also to show respect to their fellow knight. Through the years, this lifting of the hand to the brow became recognized in the military as a sign of respect to a ranking officer. In the passage in Hebrews, Paul is referring to the respect that should be given to a pastor, the spiritual head of the local church, who is not only under the authority of the word of God, but also under the Great Shepherd, our Lord Jesus Christ.

At this point, questions arise with regard to how much authority a pastor should have in the lives of his congregation. Well, there is certainly no doubt that the Bible is in favor of authority, rules, and leadership. However, we need to be careful not to overstep the guidelines of the Bible, which leads to an abuse of authority and power, something that God never intended to happen in the local church. We have already revealed the extremes of the dictatorial pastor and the puppet-show preacher, now we will examine the proper role of the pastor and his authority as set forth in the scriptures.

The Pastor's Authority

Within the Bible, we find that God has established authority throughout every level of society. In Romans 13, the Bible ordains the authority of government to enforce civil laws. In Ephesians 5, the Bible establishes the husband's authority over the wife and children, and his home. And as we saw in Hebrews 13, the pastor holds the place of authority within the local church in spiritual matters.

However, every authority in this world has established limits. There must always be a proper structure to authority. God Almighty is the ultimate authority. Our first concern as Christians should be to recognize the authority that He holds in our lives. Our body and our spirit belong to God. We were bought with a price, and we belong to Him (1 Corinthians 6:19, 20). Therefore, the Lord Jesus Christ should take the preeminence in all things. His authority should be recognized before the authority of any government, before the authority of any home, and before the authority of any church. He is the final authority. Every person or institution has limited authority except for God Almighty.

As this Laodicean Church Age comes to a close in total apostasy, the body of Christ becomes more ignorant of the word of God. We are witnessing this all around us in churches everywhere. And the more ignorant the church becomes, the more authority and power insecure pastors take upon themselves. Such men are even willing to usurp the authority of God. This is an abuse of the office of pastor and it is akin to the very act that Lucifer himself committed in Isaiah 14 in his desire to be as God. Therefore, it becomes imperative that we recognize the proper jurisdiction of pastoral authority within the local church.

The first place we must turn to for establishing this authority is the King James Bible: the final authority in all manners of faith and practice. Second, we must recognize that God gave the local church the absolute right of self-government. The local church is to remain free from the interference of any hierarchy of individuals or organizations. The one and only superintendent is Christ through the Holy Spirit; not a convention and not a church council. Third, we must also maintain an uncompromising position with regard to Bible based doctrine: *sound* doctrine. Of course, doctrinal Christianity is no good without a practical application to our daily lives.

The abuse of pastoral authority occurs whenever a pastor decides to move beyond these set boundaries. Some try to correct and rewrite the Bible with their perverted applications of Hebrew and Greek. That is an abuse of authority. Others try to establish a Nicolaitan hierarchy or council. This occurs whenever Christians are required to seek the approval of religious boss-hogs that want all of the little piglets to come and eat from their trough. That too is an abuse of authority. Such pastors are guilty of spiritual treason against the established doctrines of the Bible. God hates the doctrine of the Nicolaitans (Revelation 2:15). It is a doctrine that undermines the priesthood of the believer and robs God of the fellowship that He desires to have with His children.

Those who abuse their pastoral authority come to believe that others should seek after them for advice and guidance. In their view, God has greatly used them. Therefore, they begin to overestimate their own worth and set themselves up as spiritual gurus. In time, such men convince others (as well as themselves) that they are practically infallible. This can take on a Baptist form of popery, no different than the Apostolic See of Rome. I can assure you that the number of years in ministry doesn't make anyone infallible, but it can make a man more proud of himself than he ought to be. It is that kind of power mixed with pride that will corrupt you. Without a doubt, absolute power absolutely corrupts.

Most preachers wouldn't dare teach this to their church. Why? First of all, they don't believe what I'm telling you. Second, they want to keep the authority that they have stolen from God. Listen, the office of pastor by no means gives any man permission to meddle in another man's personal affairs.

You can't find scripture to support that kind of behavior anywhere in the Bible.

Nowhere in the Bible does it tell pastors to advise other Christians on who to marry, what to buy, or what to have in their home. God didn't set up a preacher to have authority over somebody else's home. God gave the husband authority over his home according to Ephesians 5.

The pastor's jurisdiction is limited to the four walls of a church, just as the husband is limited to the four walls of his home, and the government is confined by the geographic area that they preside over. As a pastor, I have no authority over your marriage relationship, your kids, or your house. If someone asks for counseling, then I will be glad to give him or her my thoughts on a particular problem or situation. But if they don't ask, I have no authority over the situation and no right to force my ideas and opinions with regard to someone else's personal affairs. Listen, I know of some churches that teach husbands to spank their wives if they become unruly. Now, in my opinion, that helps to explain why there are so many divorces within the Bible believing camp we're in. Nonetheless, as foolish as that kind of thing may be, it is not my responsibility to bust down their front door to come in and straighten them out.

My responsibilities lie elsewhere. I am to preach, teach, rebuke, and admonish from the pulpit. The responsibility of my church members, or those listening, whether saved or lost, is to respond. That is where you authority as a pastor begins and ends. It is an authority limited to spiritual matter. Let's look at what the Bible says about the pastor's proper position as a leader. In Acts 20:28, the Bible says,

Take heed therefore unto yourselves and to all the flock, over the which the Holy Ghost hath made you overseers, to feed the church of God, which he hath purchased with his own blood.

This admonition is to pastors. The verse instructs pastors to feed the flock and oversee Christians committed to his care. The charge requires the pastor to lead, guide, and direct in spiritual matters. To the best of our ability, we are to admonish, instruct, teach, and preach this book of God called the Holy Bible.

In 1 Peter 5:1-3, the Bible says,

1) The elders which are among you I exhort, who am also an elder, and a witness of the sufferings of Christ, an also a partaker of the glory that shall be revealed:
2) Feed the flock of God which is among you, taking the oversight thereof, not by constraint, but willingly; not for filthy lucre, but of a ready mind;
3) Neither as being lords over God's heritage, but being ensamples to the flock.

According to that passage, I as a pastor, am a ruler, but I am not a lord. It is a limited authority. I am not responsible for <u>making</u> people come to church, I can only invite and encourage. Folks are to come to church voluntarily. I can't make them come, tithe, praise God, sing, listen, do right, support missions, or anything else. All I can do is show people out of the Bible what God says to do. Whether people choose to do right is entirely up to them. As an overseer, my limited authority only allows me to a) teach the Bible – Titus 1:9, b) preach the Bible – Titus 2:1, and c) admonish people to live right – Titus 3:8.

In Philippians 2: 12-13, the Bible says,

12) Wherefore, my beloved, as ye have always obeyed, not as in my presence only, but now much more in my absence, work out your own salvation with fear and trembling.

**13) For it is God which worketh in you both to will
and to do of his good pleasure.**

This whole chapter deals with living right as a Christian.
According to the verses above, whenever a Christian hears a
pastor teach or preach, it is the Holy Spirit that works to
convict people. When a preacher preaches the word of God
and people respond in obedience are they obeying the pastor?
No. They are obeying the voice of the Holy Spirit, which is
working inside of them **"both to will and to do of his good
pleasure"** (Philippians 2:13). The Bible does not compel you
to obey me. You are compelled to obey God.

In Colossians 1:28-29, God is using Paul to teach the Bible.
He writes:

**Whom we preach, warning every man, and
teaching every man in all wisdom; that we may
present every man perfect in Christ Jesus.**

Now just because a pastor is instructed to preach, teach,
and warn every man, that doesn't mean that the pastorate gives
him a license to become a marriage counselor, a shrink, a loan
shark, or a daddy figure. It's true that I might not like the
things that some folks do, wear, say, go, etc. But it is not my
job to preach on my likes and my dislikes. As a pastor in the
place of leadership over a local church, I must continually
examine my preaching to make sure that I'm preaching the
book instead of my own preferences, or my own so-called
convictions.

There are reasons given in the Bible that clearly point out
just why church people need to follow those who have the rule
over them:

- To prevent themselves from becoming
  shipwrecked in life
  (1 Timothy 1:19).

- To avoid being deceived by false doctrine (Ephesians 4:14).
- To stay clear of cults and cultic leaders (Acts 20:29-30).

As long as the pastor rules well, his church members can follow him in spiritual matters. How do you know if I am right? In the Bible we, as Christians, are called priests (1 Peter 2:9). There is only one High Priest, the Lord Jesus Christ. We, as saved Christians, **"kings and priests unto God"** (Revelation 1:6) must answer to the High Priest, not some pastor (see also 2 Corinthians 5:10).

In Old Testament times, the Levitical priests answered to the High Priest. In New Testament times, if there is a problem in the church, then it must be resolved on the basis of church authority, not pastoral authority. The Bible never tells us to bring such matters before the pastor. The Bible does say to bring them before the church (Matthew 18:17).

All of the verses we have reviewed thus far make it clear that pastors are not dictators. If anything, pastors are to preach the Bible to prevent anyone else from becoming a dictator. It is a simple design orchestrated by God. We, as leaders in the church – pastors – are to minister to our church in spiritual things while they are to minister to us in carnal things. Pastors are to behave and act like ministers and not like monarchs.

The books of First and Second Timothy were written to a young preacher so that he would know how to act in the house of God. First Timothy 3:15 states,

> **But I tarry long, that thou mayest know how thou oughtest to behave thyself in the house of God, which is the church of the living God, the pillar and ground of the truth.**

Wouldn't you agree that a pastor must know how to behave himself if he is going to rule well? It makes common sense.

Besides, there is a reward promised to the pastor who rules well. First Timothy 5: 17 says,

> **Let the elders who rule well be counted worthy of double honor, especially they who labour in the word and doctrine.**

And in 1 Peter 5:4,

> **And when the chief Shepherd shall appear, ye shall receive a crown of glory that fadeth not away.**

14

The Leadership Problem

It's not the stars or bars you have, and not what you wear
on your sleeve or shoulder that determines what you are.
It's what you wear on your collar; the eagle, globe, and
anchor. That's what puts you in the brotherhood of
Marines.[1]

Allow me to put my on spin on that great quote: It's not
where you went to school, who you know, what click you
agree with, how many commentaries you've read, how many
tapes you've studied, how many churches you've pastored, or
how many ministries you've been involved in. What will
determine your total ministry is whether or not you can lead.
Are you a leader? Leaders are not made. They are born. They
are born to lead. Everyone is not a leader.

There is a leadership problem in today's Independent
Baptist churches. As discussed in the previous chapter, many
of these Baptists have been bamboozled by some in the
ministry who are nothing more than Baptist popes looking for
followers. You will eventually learn that all popes don't live
in Rome. Many are so-called Bible believing Baptist
preachers. In the last few years, there has been a movement of

pastors to exert more power and authority than the Bible gives them. They have taken power and abused it. That is not leadership. It is a case of the clergy exalting themselves over the laity (Revelation 2:15). As we say here in the mountains, this is a situation that God does not put too much cotton to; in other words: He hates it! Now that will probably be considered a heretical false teaching by those little popes. That's because men who lead in that fashion are insecure in their ministries. They may call themselves preachers, but they are not leaders.

First of all, a true leader recognizes the fact that THE ultimate authority is God, not himself or some other man. A true leader does not have a superiority complex. He does not attempt to make other people feel small and insignificant. His goal is not to make others afraid of him. The only time a true leader will make a person feel a little uneasy is when that person fails to do their job. Now this is not the case whenever a man is trying to set himself up as the final authority instead of the book.

Individuals who are on a mission to prove their position and fulfill their own preconceived role of power are not true leaders, but they are dangerous. Such are individuals who delight in their own sense of superiority as well as the idea that others are looking to them for decisions, approval, interpretations of scripture, etc. Such people enjoy making themselves the final authority all the while proclaiming their fidelity to the Bible. Do you realize that every cult came into being in this manner? Someone assumed the role of authority that a man wasn't supposed to have. His followers may have even given that man (or woman) a role they had no right to give them. Even so, that did not mean it was right.

Authority belongs to God and to God alone. Whenever that is not the case, you have a man-made cult. The purpose of this chapter is not to deal with cults, but here at Blue Ridge Bible Institute, we have a great class on this subject taught by Bro. Brad Gross. You probably won't find any other teaching on this subject to be as thorough. But what I want you to realize here is the fact that we are dealing with a problem that has grown up right in our own backyards. The problem is the abuse of pastoral authority in Bible believing Baptist churches. Now I believe in pastoral authority, but not abuse by the pastor. Personally, I agree with what Dr. Jack Woods said to me back in 1983; "I'm not as much interested in being the man of God as I am in being God's man."

I know the reason why this problem has grown to such epidemic proportions. It's a matter of history repeating itself. You see, years ago many Baptists jumped off the Southern Baptist Convention (SBC) bandwagon because they had a congregational government of power hungry men seeking authority. Their churches were controlled by deacon boards and committees, Sunday school superintendents, the chairman of the finance committees, the president of the W.M.U., the president of the B.T.U., the head of the Cooperative Program, et al. To many people, it seemed that everyone wanted to be a leader except for the man called to be the leader, the pastor. Because so many of the pastors' lacked Bible knowledge and a backbone, they buckled under the pressure to go along and get along in order to keep their retirement plans. This is one reason that people grew tired of the SBC charade and left it to join the independent movement. It all stemmed from an abuse of authority and poor leadership. Now, unfortunately, in Independent Baptist churches we have progressed to the other side of the spectrum. Pastors have assumed the role as the only authority and expect others to follow. Yes, many are certainly following these preachers. They are following them out to the parking lot, getting in their cars, driving off and staying clear of the church. For those who happen to stay, they must suffer the mental and spiritual deception that comes from believing a preacher who teaches that he is the *final* authority instead of the word of God.

I want no part of that foolishness. I'm not a Southern Baptist and I'm not a Fundamentalist. And based on what I've seen of many so-called Bible believers, I don't want to be a part of their *"Spiritual Police Force"* either. What I am is an

Independent Baptist who believes the King James Bible. I try to rightly divide it and then practically apply it so that my people get something out of it on a weekly, monthly, and yearly basis. My purpose is to help them grow in the grace and knowledge of the word of God. I don't have to read a commentary to know what to do or how to run a local church. I have the Bible to instruct me.

As a Baptist, I realize that Baptist churches have always implemented a mild congregational government within the local church. In this setting, the pastor is the overseer in spiritual matters, whereas the board of trustees and deacons under the leadership of the pastor are to work out the finances and other matters pertaining to the business of the church. The deacon(s) and trustees are to bring business matters before the church whenever a vote is required. I also believe that every one over eighteen that is an active member (not inactive) can vote on a matter. This should be addressed in the churches by-laws.

Women should be able to take part in the vote as well. They are members. I'm not afraid of women. However, many pastors try to keep the women under their thumb in a local church. Once again, this happens when a pastor's insecurity surfaces in their struggle to maintain power as some kind of "He-man" and macho knucklehead. I realize that only men ran the New Testament church in Acts. But I didn't say one thing about women running anything. What I did say is that all members (both men and women) should have the right to vote on business matters of the church.

The leadership problem in Bible believing Baptist churches stems from the fact that too many egotistical preachers have usurped the authority of the word of God. Like Diotrephes, many are seeking the preeminence rather than giving it to Whom it belongs – the Lord Jesus Christ. They don't know how to lead. Therefore, no one is following. Threatened by their own lack of ability, women in the church, and the desire for approval in the eyes of all who are watching their work (not God's work), they have left the sheep to either starve or to fend for themselves. This is why we need men today who know and understand what leadership is. As we have already discussed, the church was never supposed to be presided over by dictators. Therefore, the purpose of the next chapter is to discuss the gems of leadership that I have gathered over all my years in the ministry. Hopefully, they will be of value to those of you who will one day find yourself filling the role of pastor in a local church.

15

Gems on Leadership

Years ago when I was in Vietnam, I kept a journal. One of the entries I wrote to myself back then was this:

> You never know when you're going to draw your last breath. We live in total uncertainty, on the brink of the abyss, day after day. The only thing that keeps us going is the feeling that you have to live up to the demands of your buddies who are depending on you.

One of the first places I learned the importance of having others you can depend on was in a foxhole. It's no different in the Christian warfare. Dependency and trust are two characteristics that you'll come to value as a pastor. I also consider them to be two gems when it comes to leadership.

You have to know who you can trust. And you have to know who you can depend on. When it comes to trusting relationships, I can say that I know what it means to have some true friends. I have friends like that now in my local church; men whose names I will not mention. These are men that I know I could call on for help as well if I ever got in a pinch. I know that they would be there for me and do all that they could to help me out.

You also have to know who you can follow. In the years of my ministry, there were men that I always knew I could follow. Some of these men taught me specific things that I still use today when it comes to preaching. I will always consider the late Dr. Noe to be a great spiritual leader. He taught me the *art of preaching.* He led me in the ministry and helped me to strive to perfect that gift. He taught me that when it comes to preaching you must breathe in before you can breathe out.

Then there was the late Dr. Lackey who I have already mentioned several times in this book. He taught me the art of being a pastor. He spent time with me, encouraged me, and helped me to understand the North Carolina mountain people so that I was able to build a Bible believing church here in this region of the country. Dr. Lackey taught me that "men make promises, heroes keep them."

There were other great preachers who influenced me and helped me to learn that in the Christian ministry of preaching, a soldier isn't made by dress parade, but by combat. Such words of advice were not just fancy clichés. They were backed up by character in the lives of the men who spoke them. These men led me by example and I still value their knowledge, their wisdom, and their leadership. Whenever these men spoke, I listened. Whenever they rebuked me, I examined myself. Whenever they gave me a time limit to preach, I kept to my time. And whenever they preached, taught, or counseled, my heart wept to be like them. Why? It was because of their leadership. Each man knew what it meant to be true leader! I wanted to lead like them. They all gave me some great advice to learn and live by. Their words of wisdom might seem shallow to a green horn or a beginning preacher who thinks that he knows it all, but let me tell you, down the road, you'll see just how much good country sense there is behind those sayings.

Dr. Noe and Dr. Lackey are in glory today, but if they were here, I would still follow them. I count it a great blessing to have had the time and opportunity to sit under these men in the beginning of my ministry. Without such leadership in my life, there's no way that I could have come this far down the road in my ministry. Only eternity will tell of the leadership qualities that these men imparted unto this most unworthy preacher.

Now just because you've sat under a true leader or fellowshipped with one doesn't guarantee that you are going to be one. As I stated before, leaders are not made; they are born. There's an old saying that that goes "follow me or I will die alone." Personally, I believe that if you can't lead, then you shouldn't expect me to follow. My leadership qualities are sprouting all the time and blossoming into full strength. I don't want my growth stunted. So, if you can't lead, move over and give me the reigns. Leaders are not made by the sheepskin they earned to hang on their wall or by some other award given to them by their friends. A true Christian leader was once described as follows:

> He feels supreme love for one he has never seen. He talks familiarly every day to someone he cannot see. He expects to go to heaven on the virtue of another. He empties himself in order to be full. He admits he is wrong so he can be declared right. He goes down in order to get up. He is strongest when he is weakest. Richest when he is poorest. Happiest when he feels the worst. He dies so that he can live. He forsakes in order to have. He gives away so that he can keep. He sees the invisible. He hears the inaudible. He knows that which passes understanding.[1]

I consider another gem of leadership to be the privilege of responsibility. Responsibility involves directing others as they carry out the purposes of an organization. As a leader, this responsibility makes you accountable with either the success or failure of an endeavor. Leaders are required to interact with various levels of authority. No textbook model or systemic form of leadership behavior can anticipate the circumstances, conditions, and situations that can arise, nor the best manner of influencing the actions of others. When it comes to maintaining a successful church, I've found that it can be much more difficult to keep one operating smoothly over the long run than building one.

Any good leader knows that goals are important. The same applies to the leader of a church. The leader of a church should set goals that are realistic and attainable. They should also be shared among the members of the church. Some people like to use the term common goals. But I prefer to call them _shared_ goals because it is uncommon to share goals. The term "shared goals" has a deeper meaning. It suggests that you are going to cooperate with one another and that a bond will develop. Whenever people have a strong bond with each other, they both will give equally. When a strong bond exists, not all the giving is just done by the leader alone.

A good leader must learn to look beyond what his ministry is doing right now at the present moment. You have to have a long look. Many young preachers start whacking away at the ministry and when things don't blossom over night they change their calling to something they see as more productive. These are men who are more concerned with impressing the onlookers. I can assure you that if a preacher doesn't take that long look at the ministry, there will be serious consequences down the road. What we do today will set up what comes tomorrow and into the future. Rest assured that tomorrow and the future are on their way. But if you are one of the many who are always striving to achieve a successful ministry overnight as defined by someone else, you will constantly find yourself frustrated.

The only way to get around such an unhappy ending is to define your own success. The Bible says, **"a man should rejoice in his own works"** (Ecclesiastes 3:22). My passion is to minister and to lead to the best of my God given abilities. I want my people to get better every day. If we can help the flock do that, then other things will take care of themselves. I also have a personal goal to be consistently excellent in my calling. As pastoral leaders, we should strive for that in the ministry. Never reach the point of complacency where you think that you know it all. Never believe that you have reached perfection or have climbed so far up that you stand on the peak of the highest spiritual mountain. Keep pushing and keep reaching ahead. Put plans into action. Remember that the things accomplished yesterday are gone, so you must live in the realm of today and look to the future. Anyone who is always talking and bragging about yesterday isn't doing anything today.

That is why the other gem of leadership is steadfast commitment. Leaders must be fully committed to the course of action they propose. If you're not fully committed, then you need to change your course of action, for no one else will fully commit until you show them your own personal commitment and true service to the Lord Jesus Christ. Sometimes you will have to stand alone in your commitment.

If you're the kind of person who must always have someone agree with you on a decision or seek everybody's opinion before making a decision, then you should check up on yourself. That is a people pleaser – not a leader. If you can't perform with excellence in a moment's notice, then you will probably fail in the long run. I hate to burst your bubble, but the ministry isn't all about saying "I love you" and let's "hold hands and skip." No sir. I'll tell you what it is all about. It's all about getting and keeping yourself motivated. Stop trying to impress those who will never be impressed with your performance.

Here is another useful nugget about leadership. If you're looking for success, it is one thing when it comes to getting there, yet quite another thing when it comes to being there. We must remember that it is a thin line between success and shame. Success is always before us, but don't forget failure is always near. If you wish success in your life and ministry, then make *perseverance* your bosom friend, *experience* your wise counselor, *caution* your elder brother, and *hope* your guardian genius. Remember that the simple virtues of willingness, readiness, alertness, and courtesy will carry a young man farther that mere intelligence. Solomon said, **"A man's gift maketh room for him"** (Proverbs 18:16). Paul said, **"For not he that commendeth himself is approved, but whom the Lord commendeth"** (2 Corinthians 10:18). Emerson said:

> If a man can write a better book, preach a better sermon, or make a better mouse-trap than his neighbor, though he build his house in the woods, the world will make a beaten path to his door.

You must not let your desire to lead take the form of over-eagerness. This causes many to fail. Instead, a leader must be willing to temper the passion to lead with preparation, experience, and opportunity. There must also be an ever-present willingness to learn, to listen, and to grow in your awareness and abilities to perform your God given call. This is not accomplished without tremendous effort and sacrifice of other interests. You must be willing to remain your natural self and not take on an aura of false pride in your countenance. We must also remember that each of us have flaws that we need to work on daily in order to be a better leader than we were yesterday.

Men with a leader's heart learn much quicker when under adversity. Without adversity and a challenge, a leader's potential is never realized. I believe that appropriate stress is essential in developing a leader as well. If we are true leaders, then we must take the risk of delegating tasks to an inexperienced leader so that we can help to strengthen their leadership qualities. This is the only way we can help to reproduce after our own kind; preachers bringing preachers into the ministry, teachers leading teachers, and leaders developing leaders. Great leaders will usually pass their mantle of leadership on to those who will follow in their footsteps. In fact, every leader in the Bible left a portion of himself by his precursory gifts and example to follow.

Consider: Moses-Joshua, Elijah-Elisha, David-Solomon, Paul-Timothy, and many other's too numerous to mention. With that in mind, let me ask this question: What good is power if you don't have the method to deliver it effectively by setting an example for those who follow your lead?

Even when people follow you, being a leader of people can often be a very lonely job. Still, we must never seek to shrug off our responsibilities just to gain the acceptance or companionship of the crowd. This will certainly cause a leader to fall behind. A preacher can never become a leader if he chooses to ride in the rear of the formation. The words of a great coach sum it up:

> Life changes when you least expect it to. The future is uncertain. So, seize this day, seize the moment, and make the most of it.[2]

As I mentioned at the beginning of this book, I have studied preaching and preachers for over twenty-nine years. I have seen what works and what doesn't work. I have studied preaching in every detail. I have also studied church folks over the years, since my first church in Dyersburg, Tennessee. My years of experience have taught me valuable lessons.

For example, when I first started to pastor, I was taken by surprise when they ousted me after only two years. Looking back, I can see that those were not wasted years. I learned that what General Patton said was true, "Never let the enemy pick the battle site."[3] I also learned that people speak to you in different ways, whether through facial expressions, moods, mannerisms, body language, tones in their voice, and the looks in their eye.

I've discovered that another gem of leadership involves learning the art of recognizing different things in people so that you can take the proper action. This aspect of leadership is fascinating to me. To figure out what someone is thinking. To understand who they are at that moment in time. Learning people is necessary, but it is also a great challenge.

Then there is the gem of courage. A leader must be able to make a decision in a split second. Believe me, it is going to take courage to make decisions and then live with the repercussions of those decisions after they are made. But don't let a bad decision break your heart or cause you to quit your calling. Go on and learn from that experience in the ministry.

This brings to mind an illustration a preacher told many years ago about a certain train. Many people were on that train. It traveled for a while then it stopped. Some people got off while other folks boarded. Then the train took off again. It would go a little further and then stop. Others got off. Then, as it went on, there were some people that had got off earlier that would get back on. This went on for the rest of the trip. But there was something else he pointed out. Those people that got off the train and got back on were different than they were the first time they got on. They had changed and the location of the train had changed. Things were different. The moral of the story was this: stay on the train. The reason many of the mighty have fallen is that they got off the train. When they got back on they were different and they knew that you knew they were different. The moral of the story is this: stay on the train brethren, no matter what happens or who gets off.

Remember that people never see themselves or others, or even your decisions through your eyes. They see things, people, and situations in their own eyes. Nonetheless, you have to remember that they are not the leaders. They are the followers. Leaders and followers see things differently, even when looking at the same things. When a true leader looks at his people he can tell right off the start where they are standing and how they are doing at any given time. We can tell if they are doing right or if they are doing wrong. In either situation, you must learn to love your people, when they are right and when they are wrong. Your leadership qualities tell people whether or not you will tell them the truth in any situation. Although most people don't like the truth, they need to know that you will not hold any punches if you are asked for your opinion.

This means that you must learn to communicate as well as be a good listener. The problems of many people could be relieved if they just had someone to listen to them. This would allow them to get things off their chest. Here is another thing to remember: Don't cut off other people's suggestions. Learn to ponder upon what they say and their opinions and thoughts. Once again, "if everyone is thinking the same way, then no one is thinking." When it comes to accepting or rejecting the decisions of others, keep these pointers in mind:

- A person that always asks the wrong questions will always hear the wrong answers.
- There are three reasons people ask questions:
  a. They want you to know how much they know.
  b. They want to know how much you know.
  c. They really want to know the answer.
- A person will never ask a question if they aren't interested in the answer.
- When men always agree with leaders, the leader and the people meddle in the counsel of mediocrity.
- Don't insult someone unless you mean it.

Now we come to the issue of trust. In leadership, there is no more important word than trust. This will be hard at times, especially if you have ever been betrayed in the past. A leader can get a little gun shy about trusting people after they have been hurt really bad. And by the way, Christians never stick leaders in the back. They cut out their hearts.

After a church split a few years ago here at Bridgeport Baptist Church, I was reluctant to trust anyone. As a result of the split, the culprits managed to take about fifty people with them in one weekend. I found out later that they were not living for God. Instead they had been running around on their wives and engaged in all the filthy habits of the world and everything else you could think of.

Before the split, the ones who caused it had attended the Bible Institute here and had learned the book. I did make a mistake in teaching them just about everything I knew. My Staff Sergeant in Vietnam, Billy Flanagan, once told me to never give out more than half of my canteen. But I had already given those people all I had. Fortunately for me, God never allowed them to accomplish their evil deeds. But right after that time, I was meeting with my deacon and trustees and I told them that I was having a hard time trusting them. One said, "Preacher, we're still here. If we thought that the other crowd was right, we would have left with them."

I'm not trying to imply here that I'm always right in every decision that I make as a pastor. I've had to learn to admit my mistakes over the years. I'm better at it now than I used to be. I believe that this comes from the trials, heartbreaks, troubles, and betrayals over the years of my ministry. I don't believe that it is a sign of weakness to admit that you're wrong. So when you mess up in a decision, apologize in front of the whole crowd. That will help to bring a spirit of trust. To admit a mistake is not a weakness, it is a sign of strength.

Learn from your defeats. Know also that your most worthy efforts will be scorned by the peers who hate you. They suffer the most when you excel. Moreover, it seems that the brethren will forgive you for almost anything except failure and success. Learn to trust those who have been proven over their years of service to the King, the local church and the pastor. Everyone is not an enemy. No battle needs to be fought unless there is something to be won. Don't get the Saul syndrome in your ministry where everyone is a potential enemy. Learn to trust.

As leaders, you must realize that you are part of something bigger than yourself or your ego. Therefore, strive to build honor in your people. Coach Phil Jackson once told the great ball player Michael Jordon:

Find something bigger than yourself, and then give it
your all. Commit yourself to it and the honor of the team
will come back.[4]

We, as leaders, must commit ourselves to something bigger
than ourselves. That cause is the cause of Christ. If you want
to finish on top, give yourself to Him. He is bigger than us.
This will involve many things:

A. A leader always rises above pettiness and leads his
people to do the same.
B. Great leaders never take themselves too seriously.
C. A wise leader adapts. He doesn't compromise.
D. A wise leader won't surround himself with weak
men.
E. Teachable skills are for developing church folk.
Learnable skills are reserved for potential future
leaders.
F. Care more for the rewarding of your men than for
rewarding yourself. Never give a reward that holds
no value to you.
G. Be generous with small tokens of appreciation.
They will multiply in returned loyalty and service.
H. Leaders make great personal sacrifices for their
folks.
I. We must not favor ourselves over our people when
the supplies are on short rations.
J. By our own actions, not just words, we establish
the morale, integrity, and sense of right in our
people. We cannot do one thing and then say
another.
K. Always pay proper attention and courtesy to those
who are under you so that they in return will do the
same to those who are under them.
L. Reward people of character and integrity – they are
rare.
M. Be principled not inflexible.

N. Never allow yourself or others to gain fame for the accomplishments of others.

O. Never allow your people too much idle time. This will breed into discontentment.

P. A man with a calling upon his life will become a troublemaker if he just sits.

Q. You must be determined to apply massive common sense in solving complex problems.

R. You must be committed to persevere even in the face of opposition and challenge.

S. You must be willing to have resilience to overcome personal misfortunes, discouragements, rejections, and disappointments.

T. You must remember that success to your office will depend largely upon your willingness to work hard. Sweat rules over inspiration.

U. A leader without the sense of competitiveness is weak and easily overcome by the slightest challenge.

V. You must have a bucket full of emotional stamina. "Success is not in getting on top, it's how you bounce on the bottom. You must bounce back from discouragement to carry out your responsibilities without becoming distorted in your views and without loosing a clear perspective. Have emotional strength to face seemingly difficult circumstances." (Williamson quoting Patton)

W. The essential component of leadership is timing. There is no magic formula to success. It is learned through failure. Cultivate timing. Know when to do something and when not to do something. Remember there is another day. Revenge belongs to God and as it has been said that revenge is best served upon a cold plate.

X. Once honor is in place, confidence, excellence, unity and pride will grow.

Y. Having fun reduces pressure.

   Z. Anger is good if it motivates you to do something
      good.

   So what areas should the leader of a ministry concentrate
on daily in order to put these principles of good leadership into
practice? They are as follows: 1) loyalty, 2) courage, 3)
desire, 4) empathy, 5) decisiveness, 6) self-confidence, 7)
accountability, 8) responsibility, 9) creditability, 10)
dependability, and 11) stewardship.
   Leaders must have the essential quality of stewardship, a
quality caretaker. They must serve in a manner that
encourages confidence, trust, and loyalty. Those who are
under your ministry are not to be abused. They are to be
guided, developed, and rewarded for their performance.
Punishment is to be kept in reserve as a last resort and
sparingly applied only when all other attempts have failed to
encourage the rebellious to comply. Without a flock there can
be no shepherd. Without an army there can be no battle
captains. Without subordinates there can be no leaders.
Leaders are, therefore, caretakers of the interests, purposes,
and well-being of those that they serve. Strive to be the kind
of man that leaves behind him a shining testimony as an
exemplary leader and example to others.
   The greatest memorial to a departed leader is not a white
cross in the Arlington Cemetery. Nor is it having his name
engraved on any of the great memorials in Washington D.C.
dedicated to the men who fought WWII, Korea, and Vietnam.
It isn't to have his picture hanging in the halls of the war
schools. The greatest memorial to a leader is a lonely weapon
bayonet stuck down in the mud of a battlefield with his helmet
hanging upon the butt of the weapon and his dog tags dangling
in the breeze. Gathered around it are his men who are
remembering his valor in battle as they say a prayer over his
remains just before turning the earth upon him.
   I pray you will become a true leader. They are so scarce in
our day and age. Oh for men who will go to the front of the
battlefields where the action is and where the fearful and

scared are in retreat. Lift up your hands and give the command to charge the enemy. For the war is won, we're just waiting for our Great Commander to come. There are too many half-hearted leaders today. You cannot make a right decision from the swivel chair in the office. Go out and get into the fight. Fear kills more people than death. Find something worth dying for and go after it with all your strength. Keep on moving. The pain will never hit you. And through it all, learn to be who you are, not someone else.

There are three classes of people in this world. The first learn from their experiences. They are wise. The second learn from the experience of others. They are happy. The third neither learn from their own experiences nor the experiences of others. They are foolish. As I see it the great difference between the real leader and the pretender is that one can see the future, while the other regards only the present. One lives day by day and acts only on expediency. The other acts on enduring principles and for immortality.

If you are just starting out in the ministry and have a spiritual dream, or if you have been in the ministry for many years and have grown cold because of the care of the churches, then keep the following thoughts in mind taken from the life of Joseph:

- Dreams take longer to fulfill than you think.
- There are pits and holes along the way to stop you.
- The brethren will never forgive you for having a dream because a) they never had one, b) they don't want one, c) they don't have the character to fulfill one, or d) they are satisfied without one.
- A dream fulfilled is more than the dream imagined.
- Only the scriptures can sustain you along the way.

- The dream fulfilled is a vindication of the revelation   that God gave to you and you alone.

Last of all, remember the following poem entitled, *God and the Soldier:*

God and the soldier we like adorn,
In times of danger and not before,
Troubles are over and all things are righted,
God is forgotten and the soldier is slighted.
Jordon, 1612[5]

16

Closing Thoughts

I have asked myself many times, "What can I leave behind that fire, wind, rain, the storms of life and the grave cannot take away?" I've determined that it is the imprint that is left upon the memories of those I've worked with, taught, and fellowshipped with in this wonderful journey of "Telling the Old, Old Story of Jesus and His Love." My desire is to leave behind a faithful legacy for the men who will follow us, which also honors the men who came before us. It is not to contend with sinners, but to **"contend for the faith which was once delivered unto the saints"** (Jude 3).

I suppose that God gets tired of getting called down on all sides of the arguments that arise when it comes to the ministry and preaching. Over my twenty-nine years, I've just learned to let things be and let God sort them out. You never need to lift a finger to defend yourself unless you are not quite sure that God can handle the matter. Preachers, learn to wait. Wait for time. Wait on God. And strangely enough, wait for yourself. You are not static, not in any sense of the word. All of us are constantly changing, growing, advancing, learning, and moving along the road of life. If you don't have the answer to some problem today, just commit it to the Lord. Wait! Before long, He will bring the answer to the problem you are facing. One day you'll wake up and say to yourself, "Why didn't I think of that before?" Yes, the periods of waiting on God can be a time of testing and trial. But God is faithful. He will give you what you need to be strong and steadfast and stay faithful on the old paths.

In college, before my conversion, I majored in the study of history. I still have a passion for drawing out of that well of knowledge and reading the thoughts of great men of the past. There is an inscription on the ancient "Breastplate of St. Patrick", which reads:

> I gird myself today with the power of God:
> God's strength to comfort me,
> God's might to uphold me,
> God's wisdom to guide me,
> God's eye to look before me,
> God's ear to hear me,
> God's word to speak to me,
> God's hand to lead me,
> God's way to lie before me,
> God's shield to protect me.

This old saying oftentimes gives me strength to face the ministry. It helps me to set my eternal sights on being the best preacher that I can be for God. If I ever amount to anything in the ministry it will be all because of our Lord Jesus. He has brought me through many dangers, toils, and snares, and I fully trust that He will lead me home.

Faith for the ministry is like lighting a torch, a torch that passes from one person in line to the next. You can't light the torch of another if yours isn't burning.

> Pressed out of measure and passed to all length,
> Pressed so intently it seems beyond strength.
> Pressed in body and pressed in soul,
> Pressed in the mind till the dark surges roll.

Pressed by foes, pressed by friends,
Pressed on pressure, till life nearly ends.
Pressed into loving the staff and the rod,
Pressed into knowing no helper but God.[1]

This poem contains what I consider to be the pathway, the avenue, the highway, and the expressway to being a successful pastor. As such, I'm pressed to know God so that others may also know Him and the power of His resurrection. When we embrace God's holiness, we will surely find that our confidence increases, our insecurities fade, our worries decrease, and our calmness replaces striving.

If Jesus tarries, and I come to the end of my days here on earth, I don't want to ask myself the question, "Did I preach for my loyalty to a denomination, or a school, or a preacher, or a celebrity, or a movement?" No sir! The very drive that keeps me preaching the "old shoe" way on the "old paths" was the memory of those great men of God who came before us in the past. Some of them I had the opportunity to watch, hear, and learn from.

My desire has always been to stay the course for no one but those on my right hand and those on my left hand, side by side in the ranks; and most importantly, to stand faithfully for the Captain of our salvation – the Lord Jesus Christ. Until we reach the Day that we stand before Him, let us fight the battle of no compromise and reject the new modernistic ways of preaching that exalt men and scholarship over sound doctrine and the scriptures. Let us leave an example for the new recruits who will follow us so that they too can and will have the memories that we have of those faithful men who came before us and never failed to PREACH THE WORD.

Stand ye in the ways, and see, and ask for the <u>old paths</u>, where is the good way, and walk therein. And ye shall find rest for your souls.

Jeremiah 6:16

Appendix A
Textual & Expository Outlines

The textual sermon outline is constructed whenever the preacher selects a verse, a few verses, or a part of a verse as his text. The theme of the message must then be extracted directly from the selection that he has chosen to preach from in light of its context. This method is very similar to that of the expository method, however, instead of choosing a paragraph of scripture containing many verses, the preacher only uses a verse, or a few verses, and then uses them to present what is being taught from the scripture. In this section, I have provided a number of textual sermon outlines.

As you will see, I've incorporated both the textual and expository methods very closely. Each outline is constructed with a practical application in mind. If preaching isn't practical, then it will never reach the listeners ears, much less their hearts. And if the message never reaches the hearts of men, then it becomes nothing more than words on the wings of the wind, which lands on the earth without any effect. Saints need something to get them through today, tomorrow and next week. They need a practical message more than an exposition about the eighteen types of the Antichrist in the Bible or some other deep, mysterious study for Bible students. Brethren, most Christians don't read their Bibles every day. Therefore, we should strive to give them something that they can apply to their lives, meditate on, and benefit from. It is my prayer that the following sermon outlines will provide you with examples to learn from and apply in order to formulate your own expository messages.

Outline 1 – Jeremiah 42:14
How A Man Thinks Before He Goes Back To Egypt
1) Gets Tired of Fighting the Battle – "See no war."
2) Gets Tired of Preaching – "Nor hear the sound of the trumpet."
3) Gets Tired of Reading His Bible – "Nor has a hunger of bread."

Outline 2 – 2 Samuel 11:11
Why I Must Get Back To the Battle
1) Because of the Bible – the "Ark."
2) Because of the Ones Around Him – "Israel."
3) Because of His Own Kin – "Judah."
4) Because of the Brethren – "Servants."
5) Because of My Lord – "My Lord."

Outline 3 – Isaiah 57:15
Understanding Some Things About God
1) He always starts out with His Word – "Thus saith."
2) He dwells in a place – "the high and holy place."
3) He is what He says He is – "His name is Holy."
4) He gives conditions about who He will dwell with – "contrite and humble."
5) He dwells with us for a reason – "to revive."

Outline 4 – 2 Timothy 1:5
Faith of Three Generations
1) A Mother's Faith is Convictional – a "call to remembrance."
2) A Mother's Faith is Communicable – "dwelt first in."
3) A Mother's Faith is Commendable – "unfeigned faith."

Outline 5 – Matthew 9:9
A Man Named Matthew
1) His Calling was so unlikely – "Sitting at the receipt of custom."
2) His Calling was given by the Lord with a full knowledge of Matthew – "named Matthew."
3) His Calling was so graciously extended – "He said unto him."
4) His Calling was very simple – "Follow me."
5) His Calling was immediately responded unto – "he arose."
6) His Calling was an open door for others to follow Christ – "followed him."

Outline 6 – 2 Kings 4:26
Three Questions the Man of God Asked the Shunammite
1) Personal Fellowship – "Is it well with thee."
2) Partner Fellowship – "Is it well with thy husband."
3) Parental Fellowship – "Is it well with thy child."
4) Perfect Answer – "It is well."

Outline 7 – Isaiah 28:26-28
Three Ways God Corrects His Own
1) Lightly – "fitches" a small seed.
2) Harder – "cummin" a bigger seed.
3) Grind under the wheel – "corn" harder to crush.

Outline 8 – Ephesians 2:8
The Gospel in Seven Words
1) The Source of this Salvation – "By grace."
2) The Certainty of this Salvation – "are."
3) The Objects of this Salvation – "ye."
4) The Content of this Salvation – "saved."
5) The Medium of this Salvation – "through faith."

Outline 9 – 1 John 2:14
Rare Young Men
1) Their Character – "Ye are strong."
2) The Evidence of their Strength – "Ye have overcome the wicked one."
3) The Source of their Strength – "The word of God abideth in you."

Outline 10 – Hebrews 11:5-6
Enoch
1) He pleased God (verse 6) – "without faith, it is impossible to please him."
2) He knew how to please God (verse 5) – "he had this testimony."
3) He knew how to keep pleasing God (verse 6)– "Believe that He is"/walked with God.
4) He found the results of pleasing God (verse 5) – he was "translated."

Outline 11 – Isaiah 9:6
Wonderful
1) A Wonderful Gift – "A child, a son."
2) A Wonderful Possession – "Unto us is born, is given."
3) A Wonderful Name – "Counselor, Mighty God, Everlasting Father, Prince of Peace."
4) A Wonderful Promise – "the government shall be upon His shoulders."

Outline 12 – 2 Chronicles 16
A Pattern For Ship Wreck
1) Asa Recruited Himself to the Ungodly (verse 3).
2) Asa Rejoiced and Prospered from this Union (verses 4-6).
3) Asa Reliance's Are in Things and Not God (verse 7).
4) Asa Rejects God's Messenger (verses 8-9).
5) Asa's Rejection Turns into Retaliation (verse 10).
6) Asa's Rebellion Is Met by Chastisement (verse 12).

Outline 13 – Nahum 1:7
A Good Stronghold
1) What the Lord is – "good."
2) What He is to His own – "a stronghold."
3) When is He this Stronghold – "in the day of trouble."
4) To whom is He this Stronghold – "them that trust Him."
5) What comes to those who trust Him – "He knoweth them."

Outline 14 – Hebrews 3:15
Don't Provoke God
1) A Privilege – "Hear ye His voice."
2) A Warning – "Harden not your hearts."
3) An Example – "As in the provocation."
4) A Responsibility – "If ye will."
5) An Opportunity – "While it is said today."

Outline 15 – 2 Corinthians 5:14-15
The Atonement
1) It's Nature (verse 15) – "He died."
2) It's Extent (verse 15) – "He died for all."
3) Its Need (verse 14) – "Then were all dead."
4) Its Purpose: to secure life (verse 15) – "Should not henceforth live unto themselves, but unto Him."
   a-To secure life: "that they which live."
   b-To secure a consecrated life: "should not henceforth live unto themselves, but unto Him."

Outline 16 – Deuteronomy 33:3
A Privileged People
1) They Are Loved – "Yea, he loved the people."
2) They Are Kept – "all his saints are in thy hand."
3) They Are Getting Rest – "They sat down."
4) They Are Taught – "Everyone shall receive of thy words."

Outline 17 – Exodus 6:6-8
What God Promises His People
1) Deliverance (verse 6) – "I will rid you out of their bondage."
2) Liberty (verse 6) – "I will bring you out."
3) Redemption (verse 6) – "I will redeem you."
4) Acceptance (verse 7) – "I will take you to me."
5) Rest (verse 7) – I will "bringeth you out from under the burdens."
6) Knowledge (verse 7) – "ye shall know."
7) Inheritance (verse 8) – "I will bring you in unto the land."

Outline 18 – Galatians 6:7
Beware
1) A Great Responsibility – "for whatsoever a man soweth."
2) An Unchanging Law – "that shall he also reap."
3) An Unalterable Fact – "God is not mocked."
4) A Solemn Warning – "Be not deceived."

Outline 19 – John 10:9
I Am The Door
1) Simplicity – "I Am."
2) Exclusion – "by me."
3) Inclusion – "if any man."
4) Condition – "enter in."
5) Certainty – "shall be saved."
6) Liberty – "shall go in and out."
7) Provision – "and find pasture."

Outline 20 – Jude 20-23
Thoughts for Workers
1) A Needed Word (verse 20) – "Build up yourselves."
2) A Holy Work (verse 20) – "praying in the Holy Ghost."
3) A Happy Work (verse 21) – "Keep yourselves in the love of God."
4) A Watchful Work (verse 21) – "looking for the mercy."
5) A Compassionate Work (verse 22) – "of some have compassion."
6) An Urgent Work (verse 23) – "others save with fear, pulling out of the fire."
7) An Unselfish Work (verse 23) – "hating even the garment spotted by flesh."

Outline 21 – 1 Timothy 3:16
The Mystery of Godliness
1) To the Flesh – "manifested."
2-To the Spirit – "justified."
3-To the Angels – "seen of" them.
4-To the Gentiles – "preached unto."
5-To the World – "believed on."
6-To Glory – "received up into."

Outline 22 – 2 Chronicles 14:1-15
A Pattern for Strength
1) Look at Asa's Dawning (verses 1-5).
2) Look at Asa's Development (verses 6-8).
3) Look at Asa's Defense (verses 9-11).
4) Look at Asa's Deployment (verses 12-15).

These twenty-two textual outlines are very simple and elementary. It is not difficult to get these kinds of outlines from the scriptures. They are common everyday passages of scripture that even the untaught would find very simple to preach. A man that is called to preach should be able to see outlines like this in his daily Bible reading. All that is required is for you to look for them.

Remember to look for something when you sit down to read your Bible. Don't read it   simply for the sake of reading. One sin of our day is the fact that saints read the Bible just to be able to say that they completed their daily Bible reading as though it were some kind of household chore to be checked off of a list of things to do. Very few Christians read to feed their souls or to search for the passage that stands out as an illuminated light off the pages of the Bible.

As a preacher, you should look for the good and simple outlines that contain milk and meat to feed God's people. Be sure to feed the whole spectrum of those listening to your message. Feed the children, the young adults, and the middle-aged along with those with the white hairs of time. Set your sights to preach the whole counsel of God. And remember what Paul told Timothy, "Preach the word." Stay in the book instead of your thoughts.

With these skeleton outlines, all that is needed are the sub-points and illustrations. You can fill these in along with timely one-liners. Place it all between a brilliant opening and a sensational closing so that when you throw the net it will come in full of fish.

Appendix B
39 Old Testament Outlines

Outline 1 – Genesis 2:15-17, Genesis 3:1-13, 20-24
When you don't listen to God
1) They began to listen to other voices – "Yea, hath God said" (Gen. 3:1).
2) They were easily deceived – "Ye shall not surely die" (Genesis 3:4).
3) They displayed an independence of God – "eyes shall be opened, and ye shall be as gods" (Genesis 3:5).
4) They made decisions according to the flesh– "Saw that the tree was good for food," "pleasant to the eyes," "desired to make one wise" (Genesis 3:6).
5) They began to make excuses for their sin (Genesis 3:8-13).
6) They had to suffer the consequences of their sin – "In sin and sorrow" (Genesis 3:14-16).
7) They missed the best that God had for them (Genesis 3:20-24).

Outline 2 – Exodus 3:1-5, Deuteronomy 16
When God Gets Into Something
1) The Common Becomes Un-Common (Exodus 3:1).
2) Something Will Get On Fire (Exodus 3:2).
3) God Will Speak to His People (Exodus 3:4).
4) There Will Humble Obedience (Exodus 3:5).
5) It Will Be Something You Never Forget (Deuteronomy 16:3).

Outline 3 – Leviticus 19
True Holy Living
1) Holy Living: Goes along with parental authority (Leviticus 19:3).
2) Holy Living: Has nothing to do with idols (Leviticus 19:4).
3) Holy Living: Sacrifices willingly unto the Lord (Leviticus 19:5).
4) Holy Living: Deals honestly with your fellowman (Leviticus 19:11).
5) Holy Living: Will not dishonor God's name (Leviticus 19:12).
6) Holy Living: Will not take advantage of a weaker brother (Leviticus 19:14).
7) Holy Living: Is impartial in dealing with people (Leviticus 19:15).
(continued)

8) Holy Living: Will not get involved in gossip (Leviticus 19:16).
9) Holy Living: Has discernment (Leviticus 19:18).
10) Holy Living: Disregards unholy methods (Leviticus 19:31).
11) Holy Living: Always responds to what God's Word says (Leviticus 19:37).

Outline 4 – Numbers 32:1-33
A Call for a United Effort
1) All God's people must have a common cause (Numbers 32:6).
2) Putting self-interest first is a great danger in the Lord's work (Numbers 32:1-5).
3) Selfish interests will discourage others (Numbers 32:7).
4) Seeking to help others is helping the cause of God (Numbers 32:6).
5) Doing nothing is a sin against the Lord (Numbers 32:23).
6) Being totally devoted to the work of the Lord secures a blessing (Numbers 32:20-22).

Outline 5 – Deuteronomy 34:1-8
The Death of Moses
1) He Died with Strength (Deuteronomy 34:7).
2) He Died with Sight (Deuteronomy 34:4).
3) He Died while Serving God (Deuteronomy 34:5).
4) He Died with the Saviour (Deuteronomy 34:4).
5) He Died on the Summit (Deuteronomy 34:1).

Outline 6 – Joshua 1:1-9, 16
Conditions for Success In Your Life
1) There must be an Understanding of the Purpose of God (Joshua 1:1-2).
2) There must be Faith in the Promises of God (Joshua 1:3).
3) There must be an Assurance of the Presence of God (Joshua 1:5).
4) There must be Courage in the Name of God (Joshua 1:7).
5) There must be a Personal Delight in God's Word (Joshua 1:8).
6) There must be Obedience to the Will of God (Joshua 1:16).

Outline 7 – Judges 11:1-6, 29-32
Jephthah: Saved To Serve
1) He was born in sin (Judges 11:1).
2) He was disinherited (Judges 11:2).
3) He associated with the vain (Judges 11:3).
4) He received an important invitation (Judges 11:5-6).
5) He confessed before the Lord (Judges 11:11).
6) He was endued with power (Judges 11:29).
7) He received the victory (Judges 11:32).

Outline 8 – Ruth 1:1-22
<u>*The Prodigal Daughter*</u>
 1) She Lost Her Husband (Ruth 1:3).
 2) She Lost Her Boys (Ruth 1:5).
 3) She Lost Her Witness (Ruth 1:8, 15).
 4) She Lost God's Favor (Ruth 1:13).
 5) She Lost Her Beauty (Ruth 1:19).
 6) She Lost Her Joy (Ruth 1:20).
 7) She Lost God's Fullness (Ruth 1:21).
 8) She Suffered God's Chastening Hand (Ruth 1:21).
 9) She Returns and Finds God's Best (Ruth 1:22).

Outline 9 – 1 Samuel 15:16
<u>*Stay With Me and I Will Tell You Something*</u>
 1) Removal is often neglected (1 Samuel 15:3).
 2) Reminder is often needed (1 Samuel 15:14).
 3) Rebuke is always near (1 Samuel 15:19).
 4) Responsibility is not negotiable (1 Samuel 15: 22).
 5) Rebellion will be numerous (1 Samuel 15:23).
 6) Rejection is not always understood (1 Samuel 15:23).
 7) Repentance is so very necessary (1 Samuel 15:30).

Outline 10 – 2 Samuel 9:1-8, 2 Samuel 16
<u>*Kindness for Jonathan's Sake*</u>
 1) David had to forget the past (2 Samuel 9:1).
 2) David had to fight revenge daily (2 Samuel 9:3).
 3) David has to help finance a need of someone else (2 Samuel 9:3).
 4) David had to be willing not to show favoritism (2 Samuel 9:3).
 5) David had to follow God's plan (2 Samuel 9:7-13).
 6) David had to show kindness to his enemies (2 Samuel 16:11).

Outline 11 – 1 Kings 18:46, 1 Kings 19
<u>*Better Make Sure God's Hand is on You*</u>
 1) The Pressures are going to be too great (1 Kings 19:1-4).
 2) The Journey is going to be too far (1 Kings 19:7).
 3) The Distractions are going to be too many (1 Kings19:8-12).
 4) The Loneliness is sometimes too great (1 Kings 19:13-18).
 5) The Commitment is sometimes too great (1 Kings 19:19-21).

Outline 12 – 2 Kings 4:1-17
<u>*The Great Woman*</u>
 1) She has Persuasive Power (2 Kings 4:8).
 2) She had Perception (2 Kings 4:9).
(continued)

3) She had Generosity (2 Kings 4:10).
4) She had Humility (2 Kings 4:13).
5) She had Self Control (2 Kings 4:18-21).
6) She had Persistence (2 Kings 4:22-24).
7) She had a Great Appetite for Spiritual Things (2 Kings 4:23).
8) She had Much Gratitude (2 Kings 4:37).

Outline 13 – 1 Chronicles 16
David's Prayer of Thanksgiving
1) Some things that you will give to God: a) our song, b) our voice (1Chronicles 16:9).
2) Some things you will have to remember:
    a) His works (1 Chronicles 16:12).
    b) His Wonders (1 Chronicles 16:12).
    c) His Judgments (1 Chronicles 16:12-13).
    d) His faithfulness (1 Chronicles 16:15).
3) Some things we must witness for the Lord (1 Chronicles 16:23).
    a) Showing forth His salvation (1 Chronicles 16:23).
    b) Declaring His glory among the heathen (1 Chronicles 16:24).
        ➢ verse 25 – He's better than other gods
        ➢ verse 26 – He's not a dead god
        ➢ verse 27 – He is worthy of all glory and honor
        ➢ verse 28-31 – He is above all things
4) Some things that will happen (1 Chronicles 16:34).
    a) Give thanks (1 Chronicles 16:34).
    b) Praise Him (1 Chronicles 16:36).

Outline 14 – 2 Chronicles 15
A Pattern for Stability
1) There was a belief in the word of God (2 Chronicles 15:1-7).
2) There was a putting out of what he had heard (2 Chronicles 15:8).
3) There was a gathering together of the people (2 Chronicles 15:9).
4) There was an offering to God (2 Chronicles 15:11).
5) There was a commitment made (2 Chronicles 15:12-15).
6) There was a testing of the commitment (2 Chronicles 15:16).
7) There was a turning over of all to God (2 Chronicles 15:17-19).

Outline 15 – Ezra 6:14
The Secret of Success in the Lord's Work
1) You must see the work to be done (Ezra 1:3).
2) You must get started (Ezra 3:3).
3) You must expect the enemy to come (Ezra 4:1-2).
4) You must realize that there will be temporary interruptions (Ezra 4:24).
5) You must see that there will be a renewed effort (Ezra 5:1).

Outline 16 – Nehemiah 8:1-18
What is a Scriptural Meeting?
1) There Must Be Scriptural Preaching (Nehemiah 8:5-8).
      a. Opens the Book in Sight of the People (Nehemiah 8:5).
      b. Reads distinctly (Nehemiah 8:8).
      c. Gives the Sense (Nehemiah 8:8).
2) There Must Be a Scriptural Preacher (Nehemiah 8:2).
      a. Brings the Law before the people (Nehemiah 8:2).
      b. Brings his own style to the pulpit (Nehemiah 8:4).
      c. Prayer was a major part of the service (Nehemiah 8:6).
      d. The Preacher was a man of the word (Nehemiah 8:18).
3) There Will Be Scriptural Results (Nehemiah 8:3).
      a. People will become attentive to preaching (Nehemiah 8:3).
      b. People will worship the Lord (Nehemiah 8:6).
      c. People will love the word (Nehemiah 8:9).
      d. People will get gladness (Nehemiah 8:17).

Outline 17 – Esther 8:16-17
How To Have A Good Day
1) You must be spiritual enough to get past the inconsistencies of others (Esther 1).
2) You must set yourself aside for the King (Esther 2).
3) You must be aware of the enemy's Plan (Esther 3).
4) You must see the death sentence upon the people (Esther 4).
5) You must see if the King will use you (Esther 4:16).
6) You must keep in mind that the enemy will be destroyed one day (Esther 6, 7).
7) You must remember that God will reward the faithful in the end (9, 10).

Outline 18 – Job 11
Who Can Understand the Perfection of the Almighty?
1) The Omnipotence of the Almighty – He is all powerful (Job 11:7-10).
      a. He is greater than we can think (Job 11:7).
      b. He is greater than we can see (Job 11:8).
      c. He is greater than we can hear about (Job 11:9-10).
2) The Omniscience of the Almighty – He is all knowing (Job 11:11-14).
      a. He knows all of mans' wickedness (Job 11:11).
      b. He knows all about mans' rebellion (Job 11:12).
      c. He knows all about mans' will (Job 11:13).
3) The Omnipresence of the Almighty – He is all present (Job 11:15-20).
      a. He takes away fears (Job 11:15).
      b. He takes away misery (Job 11:16).
      c. He takes away darkness (Job 11:17).
      d. He gives security, hope, and rest (Job 11:18).

Outline 19 – Psalm 92
Some Things to Learn from Psalm 92
1) God works on you (Psalm 92:4).
2) God works with you (Psalm 92:5-9).
3) God works through you (Psalm 92:10).
4) God works in you (Psalm 92:11).
5) God works for you (Psalm 92:12).
6) God works in spite of you (Psalm 92:13-14).

Outline 20 – Proverbs 31
The Virtuous Woman as "The Church"
1) She is a Memorial Church (Proverbs 31:11-12).
2) She is a Missionary Minded Church (Proverbs 31:14).
3) She is a Ministering Church (Proverbs 31:15-20).
4) She is a Meticulous Church (Proverbs 31:21-22).
       a. Scriptures
       b. Savior
       c. Salvation
       d. Service
5) She is a Manifested Church (Proverbs 31:23-25).
6) She is a Mannered Church (Proverbs 31:26-27).
7) She is a Magnifying Church (Proverbs 31:28-29).
8) She is a Soon to Be Moving-out Church (Proverbs 31:30-31).

Outline 21 – Ecclesiastes 8:1-6
Discernment
1) Some things you'll be able to detect
       a. Words of God (Ecclesiastes 8:4).
       b. Ways of God (Ecclesiastes 8:5).
       c. Workings of God (Ecclesiastes 8:6).
2) Some things you'll be able to reject
       a. Mans' Words (Ecclesiastes 8:7).
       b. Mans' Ways (Ecclesiastes 8:8).
       c. Mans' Works (Ecclesiastes 8:9).
3) Some things it will effect
       a. Sight (Ecclesiastes 8:10).
       b. Senses (Ecclesiastes 8:11).
       c. Speech (Ecclesiastes 8:14).
4) Some things it will direct
       a. Attention (Ecclesiastes 8:12).
       b. Attitude (Ecclesiastes 8:13).
       c. Actions (Ecclesiastes 8:14).
5) Some things to expect

(continued)

     a. Reproach from the Wicked (Ecclesiastes 8:15).

     b. Reverence towards God's Wisdom (Ecclesiastes 8:16-17).

     c. Restraint to Following the World's Ways (Ecclesiastes 8:17).

Outline 22 – Song of Solomon 2:8-13

Proofs of His Love

1) He tells us of His coming back (Song of Solomon 2:8).
2) He tells us He is watching over us (Song of Solomon 2:9).
3) He tells us how He will receive us unto Himself (Song of Solomon 2:10).
4) He tells us encouraging Words until He comes (Song of Solomon 2:11-13).

Outline 23 – Isaiah 6:1-9

What The Prophet Saw

1) We See His Contemplation – "I saw" (Isaiah 6:1).
2) We See His Conviction – "Undone, Unclean, Unclean Lips" (Isaiah 6:5).
3) We See His Confession – "woe is me" (Isaiah 6:5).
4) We See His Cleansing – the sin is purged (Isaiah 6:6-7).
5) We See His Calling – "whom shall I send" (Isaiah 6:8).
6) We See His Commission – Go tell this people (Isaiah 6:9).

Outline 24 – Jeremiah 42:1-22

The Prophet's Ministry in Egypt

1) We See The Decree of God Almighty (Jeremiah 42:1-4).
2) We See The Declaration of the People (Jeremiah 42:5-6).
3) We See The Dedication of God Almighty (Jeremiah 42:7-12).
4) We See The Detection of Departure from God (Jeremiah 42:13-14).
5) We See The Dissembling of the People (Jeremiah 42:15-20).
6) We See The Denouncing of God (Jeremiah 42: 21-22).

Outline 25 – Lamentations of Jeremiah 3:22-35

The Yoke of Youth

1) The Desirability of the Yoke of Youth (Lamentations 3:27).
        a. God gives the yoke (Lamentations 3:25).
        b. Man needs this yoke (Lamentations 3:26).
2) The Discipline of the Yoke of Youth (Lamentations 3:27).
        a. There is a discipline of silence (Lamentations 3:28).
        b. There is a discipline of submission (Lamentations 3:29).
        c. There is a discipline of suffering (Lamentations 3:30).
3) The Design of the Yoke of Youth (Lamentations 3:27).
        a. The promise of God for life (Lamentations 3:31).
        b. The purpose of God for life (Lamentations 3:32-33).

Outline 26 – Ezekiel 16:6-14
Something God Does When He Saves
1) Makes us alive (Ezekiel 16:6).
2) Cleans us up (Ezekiel 16:9).
3) Clothes us (Ezekiel 16:8, 11).
4) Claims us (Ezekiel 16:8).
5) Consecrates us (Ezekiel 16:9).
6) Crowns us (Ezekiel 16:12).
7) Commissions us (Ezekiel 16:14).

Outline 27 – Daniel 3
Things Found in the Fire
1) Reasons for going into the fire.
    a. Ungodly decrees (Daniel 3:5).
    b. Wouldn't bow to worldly music (Daniel 3:5-6).
    c. Wouldn't worship other gods (Daniel 3:6).
    d. They caused friction (Daniel 3:8-12).
2) Resources found in the fire.
    a. Convictions (Daniel 3:17-18).
    b. Grace (Daniel 3:19-23).
    c. Liberty (Daniel 3:24).
    d. Protection (Daniel 3:27).
    e. Consecration (Daniel 3:28).
3) There was repentance involved in going through the fire (Daniel 3:29).
4) There were rewards for going through the fire (Daniel 3:30).

Notice: In the Minor Prophets (which can be hard books to understand), most deal with judgment. The following outlines will be more textual than expository.

Outline 28 – Hosea 7:13-16
Seven Fold Complaint Of God
1) They have fled from me (Hosea 7:13).
2) They have transgressed against me (Hosea 7:13).
3) They have spoken against me (Hosea 7:13).
4) They have not cried unto me (Hosea 7:14).
5) They have rebelled against me (Hosea 7:14).
6) They have imagined mischief against me (Hosea 7:15).
7) They have returned, but not unto me (Hosea 7:16).

Outline 29 – Joel 2:12-17
A Call to Repentance
1) Turn to God (Joel 2:12).
2) Turn with all your heart (Joel 2:12).
3) Turn with fasting (Joel 2:12).
4) Turn with weeping and mourning (Joel 2:12).
5) Turn with a broken and contrite heart (Joel 2:13).

Outline 30 – Amos 3:3
Can Two Walk Together Except They Be Agreed?
1) There must be an agreement to a place when walking together (Amos 3:3).
2) There must be an agreement to a goal when walking Together (Amos 3:3).
3) There must be an agreement to a pace when walking together (Amos 3:3).
4) There must be an agreement to a cost, so be agreeable (Amos 3:3).

Outline 31 – Obadiah 1:3
Pride: The Thing That No One Sees in Their Own Life
1) They were deceived because of their pride (Obadiah 1:3).
    a. Thou art greatly despised (Obadiah 1:2).
    b. Who shall bring me down? (Obadiah 1:2-3).
    c. Listened to the wrong men (Obadiah 1:8).
2) They were distorted because of their pride (Obadiah 1:3).
    a. They were destitute because of no compassion or pity (Obadiah 1:9-12).
    b. They were involved in oppression (Obadiah 1:13-14).
    c. They showed contempt for holy things (Obadiah 1:16).
3) They were destroyed because of their pride (Obadiah 1:3).
    a. Unkindness was returned to their own bosom (Obadiah 1:15).
    b. Judgment came upon them (Obadiah 1:18, 21).

Outline 32 – Jonah 1:1-17
The Man Who Caused the Storm
1) Jonah started this storm (Jonah 1:8).
    a. By trying to tell God what to do (Jonah 1:2).
    b. By going in the wrong direction (Jonah 1:3).
2) Jonah slept in the storm (Jonah 1:8).
    a. A sleeper: the Prophet
    b. A sailor: praying
    c. A shipmaster: What's your occupation? (He asked questions)
3) Jonah stopped the storm (Jonah 1:15).
4) Jonah survived the storm (Jonah 1:17).

Outline 33 – Micah 7:1-6
What A Mess We Are In
1) The Large harvest is all but gone (Micah 7:1).
2) The Love of the brethren is diminishing (Micah 7:2-4).
3) The Loyalty of commitment is slipping away (Micah 7:5-6).
4) The Longing for God's people is missing (Micah 7:7-11).
5) The Levelness of God is put into action (Micah 7:12-17).
6) The Love of God is displayed (Micah 7:18-20).

Outline 34 – Nahum 1:1
One Hundred Years After a Big Revival
1) The Overthrow of Nineveh Declared (Nahum 1).
    a. Character and power of the Lord (Nahum 1:1-6).
    b. Destruction of Nineveh (Nahum 1:7-15).
2) The Overthrow of Nineveh Described (Nahum 2).
    a. Siege and capture of the city (Nahum 2:1-8).
    b. The utter spoil of the city (Nahum 2:9-13).
3) The Overthrow of Nineveh Defended (Nahum 3).
    a. Because of a city's sin (Nahum 3:1-7).
    b. Wealth and strength couldn't save it (Nahum 3:8-19).

Outline 35 – Habakkuk 2:6-20
Five Woes of the Prophet Habakkuk
1) Woe Against Dishonesty (Habakkuk 2:6).
2) Woe Against Covetousness (Habakkuk 2:9).
3) Woe Against Building Towns With Blood Money (Habakkuk 2:12).
4) Woe Against Liquor Dispensers (Habakkuk 2:15-16).
5) Woe Against Idolatry (Habakkuk 2:18-19).

Outline 36 – Zephaniah 3
He Faileth Not – Zephaniah 3:5
1) He took away our judgment (Zephaniah 3:15).
2) He cast out our enemies (Zephaniah 3:15).
3) He removes fear (Zephaniah 3:16).
4) He delivers us daily (Zephaniah 3:17).
5) He rejoices over us (Zephaniah 3:17).
6) He gives us rest in His Love (Zephaniah 3:17).

Outline 37 – Haggai 1:2-14
Consider Your Ways
1) They said it's not time to build the Lord's house (Haggai 1:2).
2) They said it's time to build our own places (Haggai 1:4).
3) They sowed much, but brought in little (Haggai 1:6).
(continued)

4) They ate, but were not filled (Haggai 1:6).
5) They were clothed, but were still cold (Haggai 1:6).
6) They had money, but their bags had holes in them (Haggai 1:6).

Outline 38 – Zechariah 14:4-21
The Revelation of Jesus Christ
 1) It will be personal (Zechariah 14:4).
 2) It will be an earth-shaking event (Zechariah 14:5).
 3) It will be a return for His saints (Zechariah 14:5).
 4) It will be a day of light (Zechariah 14:7).
 5) It will be connected with a reign upon the Earth (Zechariah 14:9).
 6) It will be a time of safety (Zechariah 14:11).

Outline 39 – Malachi 2:5-7
What A True Man Of God Is
 1) He fears God: that is his state of mind (Malachi 2:5).
 2) He proclaims the truth: that is his message (Malachi 2:6).
 3) He avoids iniquity: that is his purpose (Malachi 2:6).
 4) He walks with God: that is his habit (Malachi 2:6).
 5) He turns men to God: that is his work (Malachi 2:6).
 6) He teaches the law: that is his duty (Malachi 2:7).
 7) He is God's messenger: that is his commission (Malachi 2:7).

Appendix C
27 New Testament Outlines

Outline 1 – Matthew 13:1-9, 19-23
Concerning Your Hearing
1) A Closed Mind (Matthew 13:4; compared with verse 19).
2) A Cloudy Mind (Matthew 13:5-6; compared with verses 20-21).
3) A Cluttered Mind (Matthew 13:7; compared with verse 22).
4) A Committed Mind (Matthew 13:8; compared with verse 23).

Outline 2 – Mark 5:25-34
The Touch That Transformed
1) We See Her Condition (Mark 5:25-26).
    a. She was diseased (Mark 5:25).
    b. She was desperate (Mark 5:26).
    c. She was destitute (Mark 5:26).
2) We See Her Cure (Mark 5:27-29).
    a. She trusted Jesus (Mark 5:28).
    b. She touched Jesus (Mark 5:29-30).
3) We See Her Confession (Mark 5:31-33).
    a. Jesus requires confession (Mark 5:31-33).
    b. Jesus rewards confession (Mark 5:34).

Outline 3 – Luke 15:11-32
The Servant
1) The servant reverenced the Father's will (Luke 15:22).
    a. He never tried to figure out the Father's will and ways.
    b. He forgave and forgot what the Father did.
    c. He never worried about whether the prodigal deserved what he got.
    d. He never worried about whether the elder brother was right or wrong.
    e. He never worried about who was invited to the party.
2) The servant was involved in the restoration of the Prodigal (22-24).
    a. He saw the Father's tears.

(continued)

        b. He saw the son repent.

        c. He saw the Father forgive.

        d. He saw the son clothed with the best his Father had.

3) The servant tried to get the elder brother to reconcile (Luke 15:25-27).

        a. He never rendered his own opinion (Luke 15:27).

        b. He service was counted the same as though it were the Father's (compare Luke 15:23 with Luke 15:27).

Outline 4 – John 17:1-20

The Real Lords Prayer

1) He prays for their Preservation (John 17:11).

2) He prays for their Jubilation (John 17:13).

3) He prays for their Emancipation (John 17:15).

4) He prays for their Sanctification (John 17:17).

5) He prays for their Unification (John 17:21).

6) He prays for their Association (John 17:24).

7) He prays for their Glorification (John 17:24).

Outline 5 – Acts 16:23-34

The Philippian Jailor

1) He was a Calloused man (Acts 16:23-24).

        a. Notice how he receives the prisoners (Acts 16:23).

        b. Notice how he treats the prisoners (Acts 16:24).

        c. Notice how he leaves the prisoners (Acts 16:24).

2) He was a Condemned man (Acts 16:25-27).

3) He was a Convicted man (Acts 16:28-29).

4) He was a Converted man (Acts 16:30-31).

5) He was a Consecrated man (Acts 16:32-34).

Outline 6 – Romans 8

A Biblical Understanding Of Romans 8:28

1) Our Past (verses 2-15)

        a. Shows we cannot work for salvation (Romans 8:3-4).

        b. Shows why the lost do as they do (Romans 8:5-8).

2) Our Present (Romans 8:15-27).

        a. Suffering (Romans 8:18).

        b. Groaning (Romans 8:23).

        c. Patience (Romans 8:25).

        d. Infirmities (Romans 8:26).

        e. Prevailing Prayers (Romans 8:26).

3) Our Future (Romans 8:29-39).

        a. After salvation (Romans 8:29).

        b. Things in this life (Romans 8:35-37).

        c. Things in the next life (Romans 8:38-39).

Outline 7 – 1 Corinthians 1:18-2:5
Preaching
1) Preaching divides the human race (1 Corinthians 18:18).
2) Preaching delights the heart of God (1 Corinthians 18:21).
       a. Against Jewish signs (1 Corinthians 18:22).
       b. Against worldly wisdom (1 Corinthians 18:22).
       c. Preaches the right message (1 Corinthians 18:23).
3) Preaching defines the believer (1 Corinthians 18:26).
       a. Family
       b. Finances
       c. Future
4) Preaching displays the glory of God (1 Corinthians 18:29-31).
       a. When the flesh is crucified (1 Corinthians 18:29).
       b. When Christ is magnified (1 Corinthians 18:30).
       c. When we preach what is written (1 Corinthians 18:31).
5) Preaching debases the Preacher (1 Corinthians 2:1-5).
       a. His Knowledge (1 Corinthians 2:2)
       b. His Strength (1 Corinthians 2:3).
       c. His Boldness (1 Corinthians 2:4).
       d. Himself (1 Corinthians 2:5).

Outline 8 – 2 Corinthians 4:1-18
How a Biblical Ministry Affects the Congregation
1) The Real Goal of the Christian Life (2 Corinthians 4:1-2).
       a. Don't quit (2 Corinthians 4:1).
       b. Be honest (2 Corinthians 4:2).
       c. Walk right (2 Corinthians 4:2).
       d. Handle the word of God right (2 Corinthians 4:2).
       e. Live in the light of others conscience (2 Corinthians 4:2).
2) The Reasons for a Christian Life (2 Corinthians 4:3-6).
       a. Gospel is hid otherwise (2 Corinthians 4:3).
       b. Sinners are blinded (2 Corinthians 4:4).
       c. The message has not lost its power (2 Corinthians 4:5).
       d. There is a great need to see the light (2 Corinthians 4:6).
3) The Revelation of the Christian Life Is Gladly Endured (2 Corinthians 4:7-12).
       a. Troubled, but not distressed (2 Corinthians 4:8).
       b. Perplexed, but not despairing (2 Corinthians 4:8).
       c. Persecuted, but not forsaken (2 Corinthians 4:9).
       d. Cast down, but not destroyed (2 Corinthians 4:9).
4) The Rejoicing of the Christian Life Granted to Us (2 Cor. 4:13-15).
       a. Faith makes us speak up (2 Corinthians 4:13).
       b. Promises keep us fired up (2 Corinthians 4:14).
(continued)

204 Old Path Preaching Methods

    c. Abundant grace keeps us lifting Him up (2 Corinthians 4:15).
5) The Resolution of the Christian Life that is Governed by us (2
  Corinthians 4:16-18).
    a. Not by the way we feel (2 Corinthians 4:16).
    b. Not by the way we think (2 Corinthians 4:17).
    c. Not by the way things look (2 Corinthians 4:18).

Outline 9 – Galatians 2:20-21
The Life I Now Live
1) It is a life connected with a Cross (Galatians 2:20).
2) It is a life connected with a Continual Battle (Galatians 2:20).
3) It is a life connected with a Confederacy of Thoughts (Galatians 2:20).
4) It is a life connected with Continual Thankfulness (Galatians 2:20).
5) It is a life connected with a Consciousness of Pleasing God (Galatians
  2:21).

Outline 10 – Ephesians 6:10-24
How to Keep Standing
1) Don't Ever Change What You Believe (Ephesians 6:14).
2) Don't Ever Change the Way You Live (Ephesians 6:14).
3) Don't Ever Change What You Do (Ephesians 6:15).
4) Don't Ever Change Who You Trust (Ephesians 6:16).
5) Don't Ever Change the Book You Read (Ephesians 6:17).
6) Don't Ever Change Who You Come To (Ephesians 6:18).

Outline 11 – Philippians 4:4-13
How To Live A Successful Christian Life
1) There are some things you have to do (Philippians 4:4-7).
    a. Rejoice always (Philippians 4:4).
    b. Forebear others (Philippians 4:5).
    c. Be ready for the coming of Christ (Philippians 4:5).
    d. Be careful for nothing (Philippians 4:6).
    e. Pray about everything (Philippians 4:6).
2) There are some things you have to be (Philippians 4:8).
    a. Truthful: this deals with our mouths (Philippians 4:8).
    b. Honest: this deals with our money (Philippians 4:8).
    c. Just: this deals with our manner of life (Philippians 4:8).
    d. Pure: this deals with our morals (Philippians 4:8).
    e. Lovely: this deals with our marriages (Philippians 4:8).
3) There are some things you have to show up (Philippians 4:8-13).
    a. A good report (Philippians 4:8).
    b. Care for others (Philippians 4:10).
    c. Contentment in any circumstance (Philippians 4:11-12).
    d. Full confidence in Christ (Philippians 4:13).

Outline 12 – Colossians 1:1-14
Privileges of the New Testament Saints
1) We see our position (Colossians 1:2).
       a. Called Saints
       b. Called Brethren
2) We see our portion (Colossians 1:2).
       a. Grace
       b. Peace
3) We see our practice (Colossians 1:3-8).
       a. Giving thanks (Colossians 1:3).
       b. Exercising faith (Colossians 1:4).
       c. Demonstrating love (Colossians 1:4).
       d. Revealing hope (Colossians 1:5).
       e. Producing fruit (Colossians 1:6).
4) We see our prayer (Colossians 1:9-11).
       a. For the knowledge of His will (Colossians 1:9).
       b. To walk worthy (Colossians 1:10).
       c. For strength (Colossians 1:11).
5) We see our praise (Colossians 1:12-14).
       a. Because we have been made partakers (Colossians 1:12).
       b. Because we have been delivered (Colossians 1:13).
       c. Because we have been redeemed and forgiven (Colossians 1:14).

Outline 13 – 1 Thessalonians 2:1-9
Our Entrance Among You
1) We do not deceive with the word of God (1 Thessalonians 2:3).
2) We have been put in trust with the Gospel (1 Thessalonians 2:4).
3) We do not mix God's word with flattery (1 Thessalonians 2:4).
4) We do not seek the glory of man (1 Thessalonians 2:6).
5) We seek the betterment of others, not our own advancement (1 Thessalonians 2:8-12).

Outline 14 – 2 Thessalonians 2 1-12
The Man Of Sin
1) His Character: the Son of Perdition (2 Thessalonians 2:3).
2) His Appearing: After the apostasy of the Church, a falling away (2 Thessalonians 2:3).
3) His Mission: to oppose God and exalt himself over God (2 Thessalonians 2:4).
4) His Methods: Powers of Satan; signs, lying wonders, and deceivableness (2 Thessalonians 2:9-10).
5) His Destruction: Consumed by the Lord (1 Thessalonians 2:8).

Outline 15 – 1 Timothy 1:15
The Faithful Saying
1) How We Preach the Gospel (1 Timothy 1:15).
        a. As a certainty, a "faithful saying."
        b. As an every day saying, " saying."
        c. As claiming your attention, "worthy of all acceptance."
2) What Gospel Do We Preach (1 Timothy 1:15).
        a. The person of Christ, "Christ Jesus."
        b. Of divine visitation, "came into the world."
        c. The Gospel of a finished work, "I obtained mercy."
        d. Of divine deliverance, "to save sinners."
3-Why Do We Preach the Gospel (1 Timothy 1:16).
        a. Because it saved us, "I obtained mercy."
        b. It is a blessing to all who obtain it, "I obtained mercy."
        c. Because we cannot help it. "I obtained mercy."

Outline 16 – 2 Timothy 2:1-26
An Old Preacher Instructing a Young Preacher on How to Serve God
1) As a Son (2 Timothy 2:1-2).
2) As a Soldier (2 Timothy 2:3-4).
3) As a Striver (2 Timothy 2:5).
4) As a Steward (2 Timothy 2:6-7).
5) As a Sufferer (2 Timothy 2:8-12).
6) As a Student (2 Timothy 2:15-16).
7) As a Saint (2 Timothy 2:19-23).
8) As a Servant (2 Timothy 2:24-26).

Outline 17 – Titus 2:11-14
God's Salvation
1) Its Need: Ungodliness and Worldly Lusts (Titus 2:11).
2) Its Source: God's Grace (Titus 2:11).
3) Its Scope: To All Men (Titus 2:11).
4) Its Sacrifice: Christ (Titus 2:14).
5) Its Effect
        a. Redemption (Titus 2:14).
        b. Soberness (Titus 2:12).
        c. Righteousness (Titus 2:12).
        d. Godliness (Titus 2:12).
        e. Purity (Titus 2:14).
        f. Christ-likeness (Titus 2:14).
        g. Good Works (Titus 2:14).
6) Its Consummation: Christ's Soon Return (Titus 2:13).

Outline 18 – Philemon 1:1-10
The Man Paul
1) A Prisoner of Jesus Christ (Philemon 1:1).
2) A Laborer for Christ (Philemon 1:1).
3) A Soldier for Christ (Philemon 1:2).
4) A Thankful Saint (Philemon 1:4).
5) A Man of Prayer (Philemon 1:4).
6) A Spiritual Father (Philemon 1:10).
7) A Soul Winner (Philemon 1:19).

Outline 19 – Hebrews 11:1-30
Faith That Is Real
1) Abel: Faith Worshipping (Hebrews 11:4).
2) Enoch: Faith Walking (Hebrews 11:5).
3) Noah: Faith Working (Hebrews 11:6).
4) Abraham: Faith Waiting (Hebrews 11:8).
5) Moses: Faith Warning (Hebrews 11:28).
6) Joshua: Faith Winning (Hebrews 11:30).

Outline 20 – James 4:1-17
Why Should We Submit Ourselves Unto God
1) So we can overcome the sins of our past lives (James 4:1-4).
2) So we can receive the grace of God (James 4:6).
3-So we can resist the Devil (James 4:7).
4-So we can be lifted up (James 4:10).
5-So we can be ready to die (James 4:13-14).
6-So we can know His will daily (James 4:15).
7-So we can do the right thing and not sin against God (James 4:17).

Outline 21 – 1 Peter 3:1-19
Peter Encourages Us To Endeavor
1) A Living Faith (1 Peter 3:1-7).
    a. Condemns our past life of sin in light of Christ suffering (1 Peter 3:1-4).
    b. Considers our future in light of coming judgment (1 Peter 3:5-6).
    c. Condition of our present life in the light of vigilance and prayer (1 Peter 3:7).
2) A Fervent Love (1 Peter 3:8-11).
    a. In forgiving each other (1 Peter 3:8).
    b. In showing hospitality (1 Peter 3:9).
    c. In holding a helping attitude towards each other (3:10-11).
3) A Joyful Hope (1 Peter 3:12-19).
(continued)

a. Based upon our partnership of Christ's suffering (1 Peter 3:12-13).
b. Based upon our partnership in Christ's reproach (1 Peter 3:14-16).
c. Based upon the presentation of ourselves to Christ (1 Peter 3:17-18).

Outline 22 – 2 Peter 2:16-21
The Prophetic Word
1) The Certainty of the Prophetic Word (2 Peter 2:19).
    a. The reality of the First Advent.
    b. The necessity of the Second Advent.
2) The Character of the Prophetic Word (2 Peter 2:20-21).
    a. It is divinely inspired.
    b. It is divinely interpreted.
3-The Challenge of the Prophetic Word (2 Peter 2:19).
    a. A searching light.
    b. A saving light.
    c. A satisfying light.

Outline 23 – 1 John 4:10
Herein Is Love
1) A Joyful Acclamation, "Herein is love."
2) A Shameless Confession, "not that we loved God."
3) A Blessed Revelation, "but that He loved us."
4) A Wonderful Condescension, "and sent his Son."
5) A Gracious Provision, "propitiation."
6) A Woeful Possession, "our sins."

Outline 24 – 2 John 1:4-10
Walking In Truth
1) Expresses Life (2 John 4:2).
2) Encourages Believers (2 John 4:4).
3) Elects to Obey (2 John 1:6).
4) Endears the Heritage (2 John 1:8).
5) Exalts Christ's Doctrine (2 John 1:9).
6) Ejects Error ((2 John 1:10).

Outline 25- 3 John
Knowing the Truth
1) Truth Is Something Known Inwardly (3 John 1-6).
    a. A basis for love (3 John 1).
    b. Motive for consideration (3 John 2).
(continued)

c. Indwelling reality of guidance (3 John 3).

d. Source for joy (3 John 4).

e. Encourages us to be faithful (3 John 5-6).

2) Truth Is Something Known Outwardly (3 John 7-10).

a. An incentive for service (3 John 7).

b. A guide for togetherness (3 John 8).

c. A discerner of schisms (3 John 9-10).

3) Truth Is Something Known Upwardly (3 John 11-14).

a. A tool for good (3 John 11).

b. Testimony to godly living (3 John 12).

c. A bond of fellowship (3 John 13-14).

Outline 26 – Jude
Contending for the Faith

1) There must be edification of the Saints (Jude 20).

a. Notice the people, "beloved" (Jude 20).

b. Notice the plan, "build up yourselves" (Jude 20).

c. Notice the prayer, "in the Holy Ghost."

2) There must be an evaluation of the Servants (Jude 21-22).

a. Command of the servant, "keep yourselves" (Jude 21).

b. Obligation of the servant, "keep yourself" (Jude 21).

c. Expectation of the servant, "looking for" (Jude 22).

d. Compassion of the servant, "making the difference" (Jude 22).

3) The Evangelism of the Sinner (Jude 23).

a. We must have a strategy for the lost (Jude 23).

b. We must hate the sin, not the sinner (Jude 23).

c. We must give them assurance that Christ can keep them (Jude 24).

Outline 27 – Revelation 3:20
The Divine Visitor

1) He Knocks as a Redeemer, "Open the door" …that He might save.

2) He Knocks as a Physician. "Hear my voice"…that He might heal.

3) He Knocks as a Teacher. His "voice" speaking…that He might teach.

4) He Knocks as a King, "Behold, I" (verse 20)… that He might rule.

5) He Knocks as a Merchant, "Sup with him, He with me"…that He Might enrich.

6) He Knocks as a Bridegroom. "Come in to him"…that He might show His love.

Appendix D
Expository Outlines - Psalm 119

Psalm 119 is one of the greatest chapters in the Bible. It has 176 verses (16x11), which incidentally points to the 1611 Authorized Version. The following section gives basic examples of expository outlines for each major section of the chapter. Knowing that these exposition outlines of Psalms 119 provide only a small portion of what the passage holds, I pray they will help you on your pursuit to excellence in mastering the lost art of Bible preaching.

Aleph
A Clear Walk
 1) Resounding to God's Word (verses 1-3).
 2) Realizing God's Ways (verses 4-6).
 3) Recognizing God's Word (verses 7-8).

Beth
A Cleansed Life
 1) A Certain Cleansing (verse 9).
 2) A Soul's Seeking (verse 10).
 3) A Heart Hiding (verse 11).
 4) A Right Rejoicing (verses 12-14).
 5) A Mind Meditating (verses 15-16).

Gimel
A Clarified Vision
 1) The Bounty of His Work (verse 17).
 2) The Beholding of His Word (verse 18).
 3) The Breaking of His Will (verses 19-22).
 4) The Blessing of His Way (verses 23-24).

Daleth
A Chosen Way
1) Humiliation: A Place of Blessing (verse 25).
2) Declaration: A Proclamation of Repentance (verse 26).
3) Education: A Perception of Truth (verse 27).
4) Supplication: A Promise of Power (verse 28-29).
5) Determination: Persistence of Faith (verses 30-32).

He
A Consecrated Life
1) An Obedient Head (verses 33-34).
2) An Observing Heart (verses 35-36).
3) An Occupied Helper (verses 37-40).

Vau
A Confident Profession
1) Liberty is a Walk (verses 41-45).
2) Love is the Center of our Will (verses 46-47).
3) Lifted Hands are the Consecration of our Way (verse 48).

Zain
A Comforting Help
1) Hope in the Word of God (verse 49).
2) Help in the Comfort of God (verse 50).
3) Horror for Those Who Forsake God (verse 51-53).
4) Happiness in Fellowshipping with God (verse 54).
5) Holiness by the Power of God (verses 55-56).

Cheth
A Crying Out of Hope
1) Precious Portion (verse 57).
2) Power Prayer (verse 58).
3) Pondering Pursuit (verse 59-60).
4) Profane Persecutor (verse 61).
5) Promised Praise (verse 62).
6) Pious Partners (verse 63).
7) Persistent Petition (verse 64).

Teth
A Compassionate Lord
1) The Benefit of Affliction (verse 65-68).
2) The Blessing of an Undivided Heart (verses 69-70).
3) The Beauty of the Eternal Word (verse 71-72).

Jod
A Consistent Faithfulness
  1) Humble Learner (verses 73-74).
  2) Heavenly Leader (verses 75-76).
  3) Holy Life (verse 77).
  4) Healthy Lesson (verse 78).
  5) Hopeful Learner (verses 79-80).

Caph
A Conspiring Enemy
  1) Acute Afflictions (verses 81-84).
  2) Arrogant Adversaries (verses 85-88).

Lamed
A Changeless Manifestation
  1) Stability of the Word (verses 89-91).
  2) Support of the Word (verse 92).
  3) Statements about the Word (verses 93-94).
  4) Study of the Word (verse 95).
  5) Scope of the Word (verse 96).

Mem
A Clear Understanding
  1) Welcome for the Word (verse 97).
  2) Wisdom from the Word (verses 98-100).
  3) Walk According to the Word (verses 101-102).
  4) Wealth Found in the Word (verses 103-104).

Nun
A Conflicting Opposition
  1) Pilgrim Path (verse 105).
  2) Proclaimed Purpose (verse 106).
  3) Prayer in Persecution (verses 107-108).
  4) Protests Amid Perils (verses 109-110).
  5) Perpetual Portion (verse 111).
  6) Pursued Purpose (verse 112).

Samech
A Certain Upholder
  1) Safe Hiding Place (verses 113-114).
  2) Strong Helper (verses 115-117).
  3) Smiting Hand (verses 118-120).

Ain

A Constraining Prayer
1) A Personal Plea (verses 121-123).
2) An Omnipotent Operator (verses 123-126).
3) A Determined Disciple (verses 127-128).

Pe

A Cruel Oppression
1) The Salvation of His Grace (verses 129-130).
2) The Supplication in the Race (verses 131-134).
3) The Shinning of His Face (verses 135-136).

Tzaddi

A Comprehensive Testimony
1) The Righteousness of the Word (verses 137-138).
2) The Refining Power of the Word (verses 139-143).
3) The Revealing Power of the Word (verse 144).

Koph

A Compassing Deliverer
1) The Need of Men (verses 145-146).
2) The Night of Fear (verses147-148).
3) The Nearness of God (verses 149-152).

Resh

A Considering Love
1) A Plaintive Cry (verses 153-154).
2) A Precious Consolation (verses 155-156).
3) A Personal Consideration (verses 157-160).

Schin

A Calm Peace
1) The Riches of the Grace of God (verses 161-162).
2) The Rejoicing of the Child of God (verses 163-164).
3) The Revealing of the Life of God (verses 165-168).

Tau

A Confessing Soul
1) Prayer Entreating (verses 169-170).
2) Praise Expected (verses 171-172).
3) Power Experienced (verses 173).
4) Pardon Enjoyed (verses174-175).
5) Possession Enduring (verse176).

Recommended Reading

o   Adams, J.E., *Preaching with Purpose: The Urgent Task of Homiletics*, Grand Rapids: Zondervan, 1982.

o   Blackwood, Andrew W., *Expository Preaching for Today*, New York: Abingdon Press, 1953.

o   Broadus, John A., *On the Preparation and Delivery of Sermons*, 1926 Revised edition by Jesse Burton Weatherspoon, New York: Harper Books, 1943.

o   Bugg, Charles B., *Preaching from the Inside Out*, Nashville: Broadman Press, 1992.

o   Farra, Harry, *The Sermon Doctor: Prescriptions for Successful Preaching*, Grand Rapids: Baker Book House, 1989.

o   Jowett, John H., *The Preacher: His Life and Work*, Grand Rapids: Baker Book House, 1968.

o   Knox, John, *Contemporary Preaching*, Nashville: Abringdon Press, n.d.

o   Koller, Charles W., *Expository Preaching without Notes*, Grand Rapids: Baker Book House, 1962.

o   Lloyd Jones, D. Martin, *Preaching and Preachers*, Grand Rapids: Zondervan, 1971.

o   Morgan, G. Campbell, *Preaching*

o   Oldford, Stephen F., *Preaching the Word of God*, Memphis: Encounter Ministries Inc., 1989.

o   Perry, Lloyd, *A Manual for Biblical Preaching*, Grand Rapids: Baker Book House, 1965.

o   Perry, Lloyd and Faris D. Whitesell, *Variety in your Preaching*, Westwood NJ: Fleming H Revell Co., 1954.

o   Spurgeon, C.H., *Great Pulpit Masters*, Old Tappan NJ: Fleming H. Revell Co., 1949.

o   -------, *Lectures to My Students*, Grand Rapids: Zondervan Publishing House, 1954.

o   Stewart, James S., *Heralds of God*, London: Hodder & Stoughton, 1946.

o   Unger, Merrill F., *Principals of Expository Preaching*, Grand Rapids: Zondervan Publishing House, 1955.

o   Vines, Jerry, *A Guide to Effective Sermon Delivery*, Chicago: Moody Press, 1986.

o   Webber, F.R.A., *History of Preaching in Britain and America*, 3 vols., Milwaukee: Northwestern Publishing House, 1952-1957.

o   White, Douglas M., *The Excellence of Exposition*, Neptune NJ: Loizeaux Brothers Inc., 1977.

o   Whitesell, Faris D., *Power of Expository Preaching*, Westwood NJ: Fleming H. Revell Co., 1963.

o   Wiersbe, Warren W., *Listening to the Giants: A guide to good reading and preaching*, Grand Rapids: Baker Book House, 1980.

o   Wood, A. Skevington., *The Art of Preaching: Message, Method and Motive in Preaching*, Grand Rapdis: Zondervan, 1964.

Notes

Introduction

[1] Dr. Carl Lackey, Sermons on the Baptist, 1986.
[2] Bounds, E.M. *The Complete Works of E.M. Bounds on Prayer*, 1912, p. 448.

Chapter One: *The Call of the Preacher – Spiritual & Biblical Tests*

[1] Olford, Stephen F., *Anointed Expository Preaching* (Nashville: Holman Publishers, 1998) 7.
[2] Ibid., 8.
[3] Ibid., 9.
[4] Ruckman, Peter S., *22 years of the Bible Believer's Bulletin Volume Three* (Pensacola: Bible Baptist Bookstore, 2000) 416-417.
[5] Sargent, Tony. *The Sacred Anointing: The Preaching of Dr. Martyn Lloyd-Jones*, 1994, p. 29.
[6] Olford., *Anointed Expository Preaching,* 14.
[7] Ibid., 16.
[8] Ibid., 16.
[9] Duffield, G.E., *The Work of William Tyndale*, Appleford 1964, p. 210, pp 172-3.

Chapter Two: *The Call of the Preacher – The Process*

[1] Lockyer, Herbert. *All the Apostles of the Bible*, 1972, pp. 122, 269.
[2] *Spurgeon at His Best*, 1988, pp.155-162.

Chapter Three: *The Preacher's Heart*

[1] Miller, Dr. J.R. *The Golden Gate of Prayer*, 1904, pp.133-134.

Chapter Four: *Preaching with Priorities*

[1] Olford., *Anointed Expository Preaching,* 87.
[2] Ibid., 91-92.

Chapter Six: *Biblical Common Sense*

[1] As told by Dr. Don Greene, Pastor, Parker Memorial Baptist Church.
[2] Olford., *Anointed Expository Preaching,* 307.

Chapter Seven: *Skills, Development, Discipline & Goals*

[1] McDill, Wayne. *The Twelve Essential Skills for Great Preaching,* 1994, p.1.
[2] Taken from *The Life of John Wycliffe.*
[3] *Spurgeon at His Best,* 1988, p.160.
[4] Jones Sr., Bob. *Chapel Talks,* 1952.
[5] McDill, *The Twelve Essentials for Great Preaching,* 1994, p.10.

Chapter Eight: *The Text in View*

[1] Gibbs, Alfred P. *The Preacher and His Preaching,* 1939, p.304.
[2] McDill, *The Twelve Essentials for Great Preaching,* 1994.
[3] Waitley, *Lessons for Success,* p.55.
[4] Brooks, Phillips. *Lectures on Preaching,* 1891, p.5.
[5] McDill, *The Twelve Essentials for Great Preaching,* p. 276.
[6] Wooden, John. *How to Coach Champions,* 1970, p.35.
[7] Shakespeare, *Dictionary of Thoughts,* 1955, p.480.

Chapter Nine: *Principals of Organization*

[1] Olford., *Anointed Expository Preaching,* 140.
[2] Ibid., 141.
[3] Ibid., 16.
[4] Ibid., 142.
[5] Ibid.
[6] Ibid.
[7] Ibid., 142-143.
[8] Anonymous. Taken from *World Bible Handbook,* 1991, pp. 597-598.

Chapter Ten: *Finalizing the Message*
[1] Ibid.
[2] Ibid., 158.
[3] Ibid.
[4] Ibid.
[5] Robinson, Haddon W. *Biblical Preaching: The Development and Delivery of an Expository Message*, 1981, pp. 115-132.
[6] Gibbs, *The Preacher and His Preaching*, 1939, p.25.
[7] Ibid., p. 241.
[8] Ibid., pp. 242-244.
[9] Ibid.
[10] Ibid., 168.
[11] McDill, *The Twelve Essentials for Great Preaching*, pp. 231-234.
[12] Chapell, Bryan. *Christ-Centered Preaching*, 1994, p. 220.
[13] Olford, *Anointed Expository Preaching,* 171.
[14] Stott, John R. *The Preacher's Portrait*, 1961, pp.4-5.

Chapter Eleven: *The Delivery*

[1] Williamson, Porter B. *General Patton's Principles: For Life and Leadership*, 1988, p.78.
[2] Thomas, Dylan. *Selected Poems by Dylan Thomas*, 1953.
[3] Ibid., 206.
[4] Ibid., 208-209.
[5] Ibid., 232.
[6] *Spurgeon at His Best*, 1988, pp. 155-162.
[7] Wilkinson, written before 1913; appeared in *Golden Bells* (London: Children's Special Service Mission, 1925). See www.cyberhymnal.org.

Chapter Thirteen: *Heretical vs. Biblical Leadership*

[1] Williamson, *Patton's Principles*, 1988, p.151.

Chapter Fourteen: *The Leadership Problem*

[1] Mundy, Lt. Gen. Carl E. *Battle History of the U.S. Marines*, 1997, p. 391.

Chapter Fifteen: *Gems on Leadership*

[1] Tozer, A.W. *The Root of Righteousness*, 1986, p.156.
[2] Valvano, Jim. Former coach of North Carolina State University, excerpt taken from his last public speech before death to cancer in 1993.

[3] Williamson, *Patton's Principles*, 1988, p.185.
[4] Coach Phil Jackson (Chicago Bulls); advice he gave to Michael Jordon who grew weary after surpassing most NBA records.
[5] Jordon, 1612.

Chapter Sixteen: *Closing Thoughts*

[1] Anonymous. Taken from
http://www.webedelic.com/church/pressedt.htm.

BIOGRAPHICAL SKETCH

 Dr. James A. Lince received Christ on August 14, 1975 at the age of 25. Before his salvation, he served in the United States Marine Corps and fought in Vietnam (1968-69). After serving in the Marine Corps, he attended the University of Michigan where he studied American history and physical education for two years. At that time, his life goal was to become a physical education teacher and coach at the high school level.

After receiving Christ, Dr. Lince left the University of Michigan and enrolled at Midwestern Baptist College. He completed two years at Midwestern, but left after he discovered their true position on the King James Bible. After that, Dr. Lince studied under the late Pastor Dr. Herbert Noe and completed one year at the Galilean Baptist Institute. In 1980, Dr. Noe directed Dr. Lince to enroll in the Pensacola Bible Institute (PBI). At PBI, Dr. Lince earned his bachelor of divinity degree and a master of theology degree. He went on to earn his doctor of philosophy degree from Temple Baptist Seminary in 1991.

Dr. Lince had various experiences in the ministry. He worked in a rescue mission and a state prison. He was the principal of an ACE day school. He pastored the Bridgeport Baptist Church in Valdese, NC for nearly twenty years. There he founded the Blue Ridge Bible Institute, which is now the Bible Doctrine Institute (BDI) located in Jacksonville, Florida.

Dr. Lince trained and influenced many preachers back toward the old path expository style of preaching. That influence and training continues through the instruction at BDI and also through the publication of this great for effective sermon preparation and delivery.